500

Tips

for

Working with

Children with

Special Needs

500 Tips from Routledge

500

Tips

for
Working with
Children with
Special Needs

BETTY VAHID, SALLY HARWOOD
AND SALLY BROWN

First published in 1998 by Routledge

Reprinted 2004
by Routledge
2 Park Square, Milton Park,
Abingdon, Oxon, OX14 4RN

Transferred to Digital Printing 2006

RoutledgeFalmer is an imprint of the Taylor & Francis Group

British Library Cataloguing in Publication Data

A CIP record for this book is available from the British Library.

ISBN 0 7494 2789 2

Typeset by Jo Brereton, Primary Focus, Haslington, Cheshire

Publisher's Note
The publisher has gone to great lengths to ensure the quality of this reprint but points out that some imperfections in the original may be apparent

Contents

Introduction

Pupils with special needs are not a coherent group, although in the past they were sometimes treated as if they were. This book aims to provide pragmatic advice from experienced practitioners for teachers who work with pupils with special needs, whether they have a designated role specifically for this purpose, or whether as classroom teachers they want advice on how best to support the pupils in their classes who are designated as such, as well as for parents. In the past, young people with special needs were often taught, exclusively or mainly, in special classes or special schools, but over the years it has become *de rigueur* following the UK Children Act and Government Green Paper, to teach them with their peers in ordinary classes, albeit sometimes with additional support.

This book is not designed to be read through from cover to cover, but to be dipped into as need and interest suggest. The specialists who work with children with special needs undertake focused and specific training for their work, which this book is designed to enhance rather than replace. However, we hope that you will find the tips and wrinkles we provide to be useful, thought provoking and practical. Certainly we wish we each had had access to this accumulated wisdom much earlier in our careers. As such, this book may well be especially helpful to teachers in training and at an early stage in their working lives, although we hope experienced staff will find something of value here, too.

The book comprises well over five hundred tips arranged in four chapters. We make no apologies for the fact that a few tips overlap, since issues and problems never fall into discrete categories.

The first chapter, **Strategies for enhancing learning by children with special needs**, contains a range of suggestions to help teachers make the most of each pupil's ability to develop and learn effectively.

The second chapter, **Improving unacceptable behaviour,** tackles some of the thorny issues that surround the problematic ways that some pupils with special needs interact with teachers and each other, and gives pragmatic advice based on long years of experience.

The third chapter explores a whole range of **Specific special needs issues**, providing advice on how to identify what these are and how to work with pupils to overcome them.

The final chapter provides **Tips for non-specialists on helping children with special needs**, including an alphabetical compendium of commonly used terms, and some strategies to help pupils with a range of particular problems. This set is designed especially for parents, carers and teachers who encounter children with special needs in their general classrooms, to help them to recognize the issues and plan ways to provide support. The book concludes with an

Information section containing some useful contact addresses, **References,** a **Glossary** of terms and an **Index**. We hope that you enjoy reading and using the book: any comments you may have about its content or format, or suggestions for other tips can be forwarded to us via our publishers for incorporation with acknowledgement in future editions.

Betty Vahid, Sally Harwood and Sally Brown

May 1998

Chapter 1   Strategies for enhancing learning by children with special needs

The tips in this section include a whole range of strategies for use in the classroom to help to improve the confidence and capabilities of pupils with special needs.

1   Strategies for effective communication and problem-solving using good listening skills
2   Suggestions for teachers of mathematics on how to support pupils with special educational needs
3   Strategies to support pupils who are school or classroom refusers
4   Helping pupils who have English as a second language
5   Facilitating the completion of examination coursework
6   Supporting pupils with a hearing impairment
7   The use of writing frames to assist pupils in non-fiction writing
8   Supporting refugee pupils in the classroom
9   Identifying pupils who are working at a significantly lower level than their peers
10   Identifying pupils with low self-esteem
11   Strategies to improve low self-esteem in pupils
12   Establishing successful school contact with parents and carers
13   Responding to physical impairment
14   Devising or modifying homework
15   Identifying strengths and weaknesses for multi-sensory teaching strategies
16   Multi-sensory teaching strategies for specific learning difficulties
17   Looking after your needs as a teacher of pupils with Special Educational Needs

1

Strategies for effective communication and problem-solving using good listening skills

Often when a pupil has a problem the need for change has to come from the pupil. As a teacher you can aid this process, but there are pitfalls. Sometimes it is easier to ask leading questions, offer sympathy or suggest solutions than to take the long and arduous route which active listening entails. The following suggestions may help you to become an effective listener.

1   **Adopt an attentive posture.** Remember that we communicate with our whole bodies. Be aware that the way you sit or stand will speak as loudly as the voice. Make good eye contact. You could also adopt a relaxed body posture and lean slightly towards your pupil in an encouraging way.

2   **Be aware of the importance of silence to good listening.** You can learn to cultivate an awareness of when to keep quiet. The pupil may need a patient listener to wait as long as is necessary to hear the problem. You can also ensure that the listening environment is quiet and private.

3   **Once the pupil has begun to talk, you can give encouragement to continue.** For example, you can let the speaker know you are listening by making small tokens of acknowledgement. You can say 'Hmm', 'Yes… I see'. You can also echo the pupil's words by saying something like, 'You are saying you think nobody likes you'.

4   **Give further encouragement to continue by giving an open invitation to say more.** You can say something like, 'Keep going… tell me a bit more about that'. Or you could say, 'Would you like to talk about that?'

5   **Try to achieve active listening.** That is, you allow the pupil to lead the way in how the problem is discussed. This could entail feeding back your understanding of the pupil's story, or how you think the pupil is feeling. You could also keep checking to see if there is mutual understanding of the problem. In this way you, as the listener, can take an active but not a dominant role.

6   **Be aware that you can hinder good listening by over direction or moralizing.** If a pupil is trying to tell you of worries concerning workload a response such as, 'You've got to make more effort' or, 'Stop complaining and finish that piece of work' may prevent an airing of the real problem and the working out of a realistic solution.

7   **Try to avoid judging or criticizing.** You may be justified in saying, 'You are just too lazy to make the effort', but it will not inspire your pupil to greater heights. Even giving a perfectly logical argument such as, 'It's quite obvious that the only way to get this done is to stay in for the entire half term holiday' may prevent you listening to the pupil's real concerns.

8   **Ensure that you don't fall into the trap of labelling your pupil.** For example if you say something like, 'You're behaving like a pupil from the Lower School, not someone in Year 11' or, 'I've never known you to get coursework to me on time' it closes up the possibilities of useful discussion and positive solutions by your insistence on having the final word.

9   **Guard against interpreting the pupil's motives or feelings.** This will prevent the pupil looking deeper into the problem. For example, if you say, 'I think you are just trying to find ways of not doing this work', your analysis may be accepted and the real reason may be disregarded. Even sympathizing by saying something like, 'You are not the only one who has found this work hard' may prevent examination of the issue.

10 **Avoid withdrawing from the problem.** Try not to be sarcastic by saying something like, 'Someone got out of bed the wrong side this morning' or, 'Life's too short to argue about this'. If you divert attention from a problem by declining to listen, it may come back to haunt you and your pupil at a later date.

2

Suggestions for teachers of mathematics on how to support pupils with special educational needs

These tips are designed for special needs teachers who do not have specialist training in maths, but who nevertheless are called on to support pupils' needs in this area. Make use of these suggestions to boost your confidence, and to enable you to provide real help to the pupils you are working with.

1   **Make mathematics fun.** This has always been comparatively easy in the primary school, but it can be more difficult in mixed ability classes in the secondary school. You could build up a store of games to reinforce basic concepts, and you could devise tasks which result in the creation of colourful display work and models for the classroom.

2   **The provision of a stimulating equipment box is an essential aid.** This could contain toy money, counters, clocks with moveable hands, connecting cubes, peg-boards, measuring tapes, coloured sticky paper and all the usual equipment required for the teaching of mathematics.

3   **Try to make sure that you relate mathematics to the everyday experiences and lives of your pupils.** For example, you could devise shopping tasks with discounts for sales, or you could plan journeys using maps and bus timetables. Don't forget that in a multicultural society, lifestyles and interests will have a wide diversity. Perhaps you could teach graph skills using the climates, rainfall and so on of countries where some of your pupils were born.

4   **Remember to reinforce basic skills on a regular basis.** In the secondary school, it is easy to think that tables and basic mathematical concepts have already been learnt. For some pupils, this is far from the case. There are readily available a number of tapes and computer games for the learning of tables. Test regularly, perhaps at the beginning or end of a lesson. You can turn this into a game and give out merits or awards for good achievement.

5   **Produce material at an appropriate level.** It may be that your school uses the SMILE resources and the necessity for differentiation will not be so pressing, although there are always some pupils who are still working below appropriate key stage levels and who will need further differentiated material. It might be simpler to visit your local primary school to borrow resources, or to ask for ideas to make your own resources for your most needy pupils.

6   **Encourage keyboard and computer skills.** There are many good commercial packages which are suitable for the teaching and reinforcing of basic number work. Many of them are good fun, too, and can be offered as an incentive for slow learners.

7   **Teach proficiency and familiarity with calculators by use of the SMILE calculator activity book.** Some of these activities require pupils to key in certain sums whose answers, when turned upside down, spell out words. For example, 'Mystery 3751' reads Mystery Isle when held upside down and leads the pupils on a mathematical treasure hunt. Pupils can also work in pairs devising sums and questions which will give the answer to say, 663, which reads 'egg' upside down. For example, I had 329+334 for my breakfast today. There are many variations on this game.

8   **Remember to teach the vocabulary of mathematics.** Pupils who have difficulty remembering key words can be set homework on this theme and also be given vocabulary books to write down words new to them. You can also make good displays for the wall with key words and pictures. If you work in a multicultural classroom, you can produce key words in appropriate languages. For some of your bilingual pupils, the acquisition of a mathematical vocabulary may be their only need as their mathematical skills may already be excellent.

9   **Help pupils to practise the skills of mental arithmetic on a regular basis.** Don't assume that this is too difficult for slow learners. Just be sure to start from an appropriate level. You may have noticed that pupils who have learning difficulties are often very competent when working out what their pocket money will buy. This is because they first of all have an interest and secondly they get plenty of practice. These are good starting points for mathematics in the classroom.

10 **Make sure that all pupils have regular homework at the right level.** Many pupils with learning difficulties actually love their maths homework. It is a subject which is highly structured and, like training for athletics, it improves with constant practice and repetition. You can give rewards and lots of encouragement for completed homework and you can record progress publicly on classroom wall charts.

11 **Encourage pupils to become independent of their memory.** In pupils with learning difficulties, this can be a big problem. Rather, concentrate on encouraging pupils to work their own way through problems. For instance, the pupil who cannot remember 6x5, may write down 6 five times and add up the numbers. You can also reduce on the photocopier, tables or number squares to a size that will fit pockets or pencil cases.

12 **If you have a number of pupils with learning difficulties, try to obtain extra help in the classroom.** This can be sought from either the school's support department, the peripatetic learning support teachers or from classroom helpers. This greatly reduces the waiting time of pupils with basic queries and frees you, as the expert, to attend to more pressing needs.

3

Strategies to support pupils who are school or classroom refusers

This problem is more common than many people realize, and teachers need to use all their powers of tact, persuasion and strategic thinking to help pupils overcome this particular hurdle. These tips are designed to help pupils (and their parents) to overcome difficulties and move towards resuming more normal attendance patterns.

1   **If a pupil has been identified as suffering from school phobia or selective classroom refusal, it helps if you can find a pattern of absence.** For example, the absence may be affected by the time of day, the subject or the teacher of the lesson. You can assist in identification by keeping scrupulous records of non-attendance. You can also check with colleagues on their perceptions of the problem.

2   **When your pupil is present, be welcoming and friendly.** Try not to be judgemental about past absence. You can show your pleasure at their return. Be sensitive to the difficulty of this situation for your pupil and don't create extra stress, such as battling over the removal of coats or insisting that they sit where you decree. Small and routine issues like this can provide the flashpoint for another departure.

3   **Discuss the situation with the pupil as soon as possible.** You can suggest ways in which the school can help. For instance, it may be possible to arrange a staggered return to normality by excusal from lessons which the pupil finds it too difficult to attend. The pupil can be invited to agree to a voluntary imposition of an internal attendance report. This will at the very least provide the school with knowledge of where the main difficulties lie.

4   **Try to avoid being manipulated into agreeing to unworkable conditions.** These might include the pupil agreeing to work only outside the classroom, or to complete only selected tasks. This may seem to be a step in the right direction, but is more likely to be a way of diverting attention from the problem.

5   **Lend a sympathetic ear when listening to the problem.** You may need professional expertise from other sources to provide effective counselling, but you may be the recipient of some revealing information which you can pass on to others. Very often the pupil will explain classroom refusal on quite trivial grounds such as, 'I haven't done my homework' or, 'I don't like History'. You could suggest to the pupil that you think something else might be worrying them, and then offer to help to sort out the problem or find someone else who can.

6   **Enlist the help of sympathetic pupils where possible to facilitate a return to the classroom.** You could perhaps let these pupils know that their fellow pupil is in need of some support and a warm welcome back. Perhaps you should warn your pupils that their kindness may be rejected and provide them with some strategies to cope with that.

7   **Remember that the role of the parents and carers in this problem is crucial.** If it is at all possible, try to enlist their help and support in getting their pupil to school. You may, of course, discover that the home situation is actually contributing to the problem, in which case this is much more the province of other professionals in outside agencies. Some parents, however, may be glad to be telephoned whenever their child fails to get to school and may have some strategies to help with that.

8   **Seek the help and advice of pastoral staff in the school.** A problem of this severity is obviously their responsibility, but they may be glad of your interest and may know best how to use your offers of help. Your records, at the very least, will help to provide a full picture of the problem.

9   **Make it as easy as possible for pupils to make up lost time.** Your pupil will naturally have missed a good deal of the work of your class, so you could provide potted versions of essential information, or you could make it possible for resources to be taken home for private study. Be aware of the possibility that such materials may not be returned to you and do not lend anything irreplaceable. However, your actions may just provide a continuing link with school or establish for the pupil that they are of concern to the teacher.

10 **Encourage the pupil to seek out sanctuaries at difficult times, such as breaks and lunch times.** This may involve use of the school library, or attendance at homework or activity clubs. The relaxed and informal atmosphere might well be therapeutic and may encourage the pupil to open up to staff about their problems.

4

Helping pupils who have English as a second language

Increasingly, teachers are likely to find that they have pupils in their classes who are fluent in one or more languages, but whose first language is not English. This set of tips is designed to enable you to help pupils to make the transition into fluency in English, which may be their principal or only special need.

1 **Create a welcoming environment.** Check that you know how to pronounce your pupil's name. Introduce the pupil to the class. You could practise a few phrases in each other's language. Perhaps you could find an opportunity to use the globe to find the country the pupil comes from. Make sure you reassure the pupil (through an interpreter, if necessary) that many other pupils have been in the same situation.

2 **Respect the pupil's space.** Give your pupil time to settle in. A silent or receptive period is quite normal in the first stage of acquiring a second language. Be aware of the educational value of focusing on the mother tongue and do not advocate the use of English only at school or home.

3 **Think carefully about where you will place your pupil in the class.** Pair the pupil with a responsive, caring pupil who can act as a good role model, explain procedures and guide the pupil around the school. Place the pupil in close proximity to others who share the same language, but be careful not to create closed community groups.

4 **Make good use of visual materials.** You could perhaps label everyday objects in the classroom using bilingual labels, if possible. You could also put up posters and artefacts from various cultures. Make sure you change visual displays to coincide with class subjects and topics or festivals.

5   **Where possible, provide reading materials in dual languages and mother tongue.** If you can, ensure that they are amply illustrated. You could also make sure that your pupil has access to dictionaries. These may be available in many schools from bilingual support staff. Perhaps you could also get hold of some dual language tapes from schools' library services.

6   **Prepare differentiated materials for use in class.** You can identify and present key words in a box at the top of worksheets, on the board, on a poster or underlined in text. Make sure you draw attention to them and build them into testing. Familiarize yourself with the wide range of differentiated activities which could include Cloze work, guided sentence paragraph writing, sequencing, ranking, circling, highlighting, underlining, diagram completion, true/false statements and many more.

7   **Liaise regularly with bilingual support teachers.** You can ask for advice and suggestions for work activities. They are probably able to help with the loan of materials. It might also be possible to ask such teachers to take your class on occasions, so that you can work individually with a particular pupil.

8   **Look out for opportunities to widen your pupil's learning experience.** For instance, if you are asked to help with a spelling, there might be an opportunity to explain a general rule, such as 'i before e except after c', or that in English, 'u always follows q'. Another aid to building up vocabulary is to get the pupil to keep a vocabulary notebook of newly learnt words and to check regularly for recall and comprehension.

9   **Encourage active participation and collaboration.** One way to do this is to set up small-group task oriented situations, where pupils of varying language abilities interact with each other and can 'talk while doing'. You can also make sure that bilingual pupils are involved in routine responsibilities, such as collecting the register, giving out books or taking messages.

10 **Be aware of the range of ability amongst bilingual pupils.** Having English as a second language is not in itself a learning difficulty, and many pupils will have reached high standards of education in their own countries. You can ensure that pupils know that their bilingualism is valued as a special achievement. Let your pupils know how much you respect their efforts to achieve fluency.

5
Facilitating the completion of examination coursework

Overseeing examination coursework for pupils with special needs offers teachers a particular set of challenges that these tips aim to address. Coursework tends to demand planning ahead, regular inputs of activity over a period of time and good time management skills, and these are often particularly difficult for students with erratic attendance or difficulties in organising their studies.

1   **Provide models of good coursework.** Show pupils what they are expected to achieve. You can do this by arranging a lead lesson which can be shared with other groups. You might have samples of past work from a range of grades which you can use to demonstrate what is required. Or, perhaps, you can introduce some ideas and strategies for their own projects.

2   **Inform pupils of deadlines well in advance.** Display these dates clearly in the classroom, perhaps using a weekly countdown device. You could also make a large and eye-catching chart containing pupils' names and the titles of each piece of coursework. Provide coloured stickers to indicate completion. Follow up tardy pupils regularly.

3   **Ensure the safe keeping of completed work.** Work should be kept in a very secure place and preferably not in the classroom. If students have to take an unfinished piece of work away for completion, photocopy it if at all possible. Never assume that because a piece of work has been painfully and slowly produced it will necessarily be kept safe.

4   **Avoid setting coursework as ongoing homework.** This may work satisfactorily with able and well-motivated pupils, but for those with learning difficulties it may be disastrous. It enables lengthy postponement and the giving of false assurances that they are on schedule. You could set aside a weekly spot in lessons for checking, recording and advising on coursework.

5   **Develop strategies to facilitate coursework.** For example, if your student has to compare two characters in a play or novel, you could provide lists of suggestions for them to tick if relevant. You could also use Cloze type frameworks to provide information to begin, say, a consideration of the possible causes of the Second World War. If your pupil is going to use a questionnaire to gather information, you could provide a working model and advise on possible pitfalls.

6   **Encourage the use of computing facilities to aid good presentation.** However, you should first check against the possibility that coursework has to be handwritten. You could, perhaps, book several lessons in the computing room for this purpose. Be careful, however, about allowing pupils to spend too long on presentation at the expense of content.

7   **Involve parents in the completion of coursework.** Of course, this does not mean that parents should help in the production of the work, but they should be informed about deadlines and asked for their cooperation in urging pupils to complete. Possibly they can impose effective sanctions.

8   **Set up regular coursework 'surgeries' during lunch times or after school.** You could establish a rota system with other colleagues which would minimize your time commitment. Make sure that these times are well advertized in assemblies, registration and tutorial periods and on classroom walls.

9   **Liaise with SEN and support staff.** Keep specialist staff, who may have good relationships with your pupils, well informed about their coursework demands. It may be possible for this work to be supported during individual withdrawal lessons. Inform staff as to how much support is acceptable.

10   **Be aware of coursework fatigue.** Although your main priority is for completion of coursework on schedule, there may be times when everybody needs a break. Try to make your class lessons at these times especially stimulating, or take the opportunity to show an appropriate video. If it can be made relevant to the coursework in hand, so much the better. Offer some incentives for a class celebration at the end of the coursework within your restrictions of time and expense.

6

Supporting pupils with a hearing impairment

Pupils who cannot hear well in class are sometimes seen as difficult, inattentive or even outright disobedient. Problems particularly arise when teachers don't know about hearing problems, or forget that this might be the cause of a pupil failing to respond to a question or an instruction. Loss of hearing is not an absolute matter either, and you may well have pupils who have intermittent hearing loss due to glue ear, asthma, allergies and other, sometimes hidden, ailments. These tips are designed to help you to recognize the issues and do what you can to assist pupils with hearing impairments to participate fully in classwork.

1   **Consult Individual Education Plans when you know or suspect hearing loss.** This is your starting point for information; it will describe the level of hearing loss where identified, and should include advice to teachers and targets for pupils. It may also give you a contact number for the specialist teacher who is responsible for this aspect of your pupil's school life.

2   **Ensure that pupils who find it difficult to hear sit in good listening positions.** This may not necessarily mean under your nose at the front of the class. Make sure your pupil has good eye contact with you and has good sight lines to the board. The pupil should sit in an individually appropriate hearing range. You should soon become aware if this is not adequate.

3   **Be sensitive to the noise level in the classroom.** Pupils who wear hearing aids may suffer discomfort if the noise level is too high. Instructions and information may be missed or distorted in a noisy classroom. Check if your pupil is happy with the general level of background noise, and take action if it is causing undue problems.

4　**Check that your pupil always wears his/her hearing aid.** Make sure you do this in a sensitive manner. Some pupils, particularly in adolescence, may refuse to wear their aids. Try to reassure the pupil and stress the benefits. If you are not successful, let your SENCO know about the problem. Perhaps parents or specialist staff should be informed.

5　**Pay good attention to your own diction and classroom delivery.** You do not need to shout, but can help hearing-impaired pupils greatly by articulating distinctly. Enunciate clearly and make sure your pupil can see your lips. Do not speak while you are writing on the board, unless you are also writing what you are saying. If you read from text, hold the book away from your face.

6　**Be aware that you may need to wear a connecting aid to your pupil.** Make sure that you know how to use this equipment in advance. Remind your pupil to give you your part on arrival at your lesson. Warning: do not visit the toilet whilst wearing your microphone unless you wish to entertain your student with the sound effects or your conversation!

7　**Make good use of visual aids in the classroom.** Keep an up-to-date vocabulary list for each new topic. You can also supply your pupils with small vocabulary notebooks. Use pictures and diagrams to illustrate subject material.

8　**Check on literacy and oral skills.** Having a hearing impairment does not affect one's intelligence, but it may have led to delays in learning and difficulties with speech. Encourage oral participation in class. If necessary provide structured literacy work. Hearing impaired pupils often require practice with blends such as spl, spr, tw, tr, ch, sh, and so on. It may also give you clues to hearing loss.

9　**Be aware of your pupil's need to read aloud.** Encourage shy pupils to participate in this activity. One way to get this started is to get your pupil to practise with you in the knowledge that you will ask them to read from this known text during a mutually agreed lesson. You can also ensure that the listening skills of the other pupils are employed to help and not to hinder this pupil.

10　**Use your pupil's skills and knowledge to increase self-confidence.** For example, in a science lesson on the subject of sound, your pupil may know a great deal about the working of the ear and can offer insights and knowledge to the group on the subject of sound. Think of other ways in which you can boost self-esteem and self-confidence.

7

The use of writing frames to assist pupils in non-fiction writing

Writing frames are invaluable aids to help pupils to develop confidence in their writing abilities and to ensure that they all achieve some success in writing. By providing a skeleton outline on which pupils can build, using key words and phrases, you can help them to concentrate on communicating what they want to say, rather than getting lost in the format.

1   **Understand the aims and use of writing frames.** You can use these devices for pupils who are not yet able to produce independent non-fiction writing. The aim is for the pupil to outgrow this useful prop and move step by step to independent writing. Once pupils have grasped the format, they can add to or reject parts of the frames, which are intended as flexible aids and not rigid structures.

2   **Be aware how writing frames can aid writing.** You can offer pupils a structure which gives them a sense of what they are writing. You can teach pupils to use personal pronouns, thus encouraging identification with their work. You can avoid presenting pupils with a blank piece of paper for a starting point.

3   **Familiarize yourself with resources that have already been produced.** The EXEL Writing Frames booklet (see Information Section) is an excellent resource that comes with photocopiable sheets. When you have absorbed the techniques, you can devise frames to suit your own individual needs in your unique subject area.

4   **Teach your pupils how to write by your own good practice.** First you will have to guide the pupil in the use of writing frames by discussion and example. Some pupils may need many preliminary oral sessions, and you may have to act as a scribe until they are ready to attempt their own work.

5   **Be careful to integrate the use of writing frames into topic based lessons.** The frame is merely a guide and is never a purpose for writing. Do not teach this strategy in study skills lessons. You might initially need to produce large size versions of frames for use in the demonstration stage.

6   **Use frames to enable pupils to recount events.** This type of writing is meant to inform and entertain. It is usually written in the past tense, in chronological order, and focuses mainly on 'doing' clauses. A very simple frame could begin, 'I enjoyed our visit to... I learnt that... I also found out... Another thing I discovered was... The thing I enjoyed most was...'

7   **Devise frames for use in reporting or describing the way things are.** Often pupils are asked to compare and contrast. As a preliminary aid, you could devise charts with two columns in which characteristics could be compared. A good example would be 'My Life' and 'A Roman's Life'. Now you can continue with frames such as, 'Although... and... are not the same they are alike in some ways. For instance, ... has...while... has ... They are also different in that... Another difference is... Finally...'

8   **Teach pupils how to explain processes in a series of logical steps using causal conjunctions such as because, therefore.** A frame could go like this: 'There are several reasons for... One explanation is... The evidence for this is... A further explanation is... The most likely one is...'

9   **Use frames to assist pupils to describe procedures.** These are written in the present tense in a series of sequenced steps using imperatives (do this, do that). A frame could be devised like this: 'How to... You will need ... First you... Then you... Next... Finally...'

10   **Use frames to assist writing which is designed to discuss and persuade.** As with comparisons, you might start with columns of say, 'Arguments for' and 'Arguments against'. A frame could now proceed: 'The issue we are discussing is... The arguments for are... The arguments against are... After looking at all the arguments, I think... Because...' More sophisticated frames can be produced when appropriate.

8

Supporting refugee pupils in the classroom

Some schools are unlikely ever to accommodate refugee pupils in their classes, while in others, the presence of refugees is a daily fact of life. This set of tips is designed to give some guidance on how best to induct, welcome and support pupils who may be seriously traumatized and certainly will need extra help to make sense of a very different world from that which they have left behind.

1   **Carry out welcome procedures.** Check that your pupil has received a simple plan of the school, knows the name of the class teacher and has a copy of the timetable. Introduce the pupil to your class. Make sure you can say the pupil's name correctly. Check that your pupil can pronounce your name too. Write it down in your pupil's book.

2   **Be sensitive to the placing of the pupil in your class.** Try to seat your pupil next to a sympathetic friend and preferably one who speaks the same language. If your school has a 'buddy' scheme or befriending system, find out the name of the designated person and, if necessary, prompt the relevant pupil to be conscientious about responsibilities.

3   **Establish basic communication links as quickly as possible.** Talk individually to your pupil as often as you can. Teach useful phrases and greetings and make sure your pupil gets daily opportunities to practise these. Use other pupils to interpret, if possible, and to repeat the information back to your pupil in English. Speak clearly and slowly. Try to control the noise level in the classroom.

4   **Provide visual support as often as possible.** When producing differentiated work, use visual aids such as diagrams, flash cards and illustrated glossaries for reference. You could write key words on display charts with translations which can be provided by English as a Second Language (ESL) teachers or language centres. You can also ask for the provision of bilingual dictionaries.

5   **Create an active and participatory role for the pupil.** Don't allow language difficulties to prevent full integration of your pupil into the life of the class. It is quite easy to involve pupils very quickly in the distribution of books and equipment. This will ensure verbal contact with other pupils. Other small tasks can be used to include your pupil.

6   **Seek out bilingual texts.** Ask the school librarian what is available. You can also contact school loans services and language centres for loans. The Refugee Council in London (see Information Section) and other major cities are also willing to provide material.

7   **Provide differentiated materials and devise strategies to aid comprehension.** Reading material can be made more accessible by oral discussion, role play, illustrations and use of audio-tape. If you can record reading material on cassette, a pupil can listen and read simultaneously. Instructions in worksheets should be clear and should always follow the same format. You could also provide individual vocabulary lists in each lesson or display them on the wall.

8   **Create opportunities for pupils to communicate their experiences.** It might be possible in a lesson, where the subject lends itself to discussion of global issues, to incorporate the pupil's own experiences and knowledge into a group discussion. Be careful not to press a reluctant pupil, but it may be beneficial for a pupil to talk about the reasons for their leaving home and country.

9   **Ensure that pupils receive emotional support if necessary.** They will almost certainly have experienced a great many stressful life events. Try to create time to listen. You could also suggest that pupils begin to put together autobiographical scrapbooks or picture books which relate to their past life. Role play and drama may also help to develop group understanding of complex events and feelings.

10   **Inform pupils of 'safe' places in the school.** English schools are large and noisy places to a refugee pupil. You could provide, or direct, a pupil to a quiet space that would give a retreat at breaks and lunch times.

9

Identifying pupils who are working at a significantly lower level than their peers

Pupils who are not keeping up with the rest of the class can be disruptive, alienated and difficult to teach. Working out where the problems lie is the first stage in putting together a plan of action to help such pupils to become better integrated and to work towards more realistic personal goals. These suggestions are designed to help you do so.

1   **Watch for an unusual level of dependency.** This may include the need for constant reassurance that work is being done correctly. Pupils may be unable to get started on any task without prompting or encouragement. Pupils may need constant repetition of instructions, and may become tearful or distressed if they think the work is too difficult.

2   **A negative self-image should alert you to possible learning difficulties.** Pupils may take no pride in any work or achievement and may even abuse or destroy their own work. They may seem to have no real friends and prefer to sit and work alone. Attempts to break this pattern may be resisted.

3   **Watch for a poor attention span.** There may be difficulties in listening to the briefest and simplest of instructions. Pupils may even fail to engage in any listening at all. For instance, they may be doodling, or making paper darts or picking up materials which are not relevant to your lesson. They may attempt to talk or distract others. They may be frequently off task and often out of their seat.

4   **Anti-social behaviour in the classroom often indicates the existence of learning difficulties.** Pupils may be constantly late to lessons or may leave without asking permission. There is often a marked lack of respect for other pupils' work or property and, in extreme cases, stealing may occur. Cheating or copying in tests may indicate difficulties with work.

5   **Reluctance to read aloud or to deal with classroom texts should alert you to problems.** Poor spelling and inadequate knowledge of semantics are further indicators. Pupils may find it difficult to extract information from text or be unable to identify key ideas in the text.

6   **Be aware of inability to express ideas or articulate a response.** Expressive writing may present serious problems for a pupil who is unable to sequence adequately, or who has not grasped the formal structures of writing or who lacks the vocabulary to express thoughts and ideas in writing.

7   **Watch out for poor organizational skills.** Pupils may arrive at lessons without appropriate equipment. Often they will have no idea where their next lesson will be. Homework is never written down and is rarely completed. Classwork is left on the desk without a name to identify it. Help with organizational strategies may be declined.

8   **Be aware of consistently poor presentation of work.** Handwriting may be poorly formed. There may be confusion over upper and lower case letters. Diagrams, tables, graphs and drawings will frequently be badly planned and executed. Rulers and other aids will not be employed to improve work. Labelling of diagrams and drawings may be illegible and inaccurate.

9   **Watch out for difficulties in number work.** Basic concepts in mathematics are likely to be poorly understood. Facility with tables will be severely limited. Problem solving may also relate to difficulties in reading text and instructions.

10   **Self-marginalization in the classroom is often a cry for help.** Pupils may be reluctant or unable to participate orally and may become distressed or uncooperative if pressed. Alternatively, they may take on the role of class clown to divert attention from their difficulties.

10

Identifying pupils with low self-esteem

Students with low esteem often punish themselves and those around them. The causes of low self-esteem are many, and you can't expect to solve them all single-handedly. However, here are some ideas you can use to establish which pupils are experiencing problems in this area, which can then help you decide about the steps you can take.

1   **Watch out for pupils who put themselves down.** Self-denigration is a characteristic of such pupils who will persistently refer to themselves, or the group in which they have been placed, in a negative manner. This may also extend to indiscriminate criticism of the school or teachers in general and an often expressed wish to change schools.

2   **Look out for quick anger.** Sudden, inexplicable flashes of anger may indicate a pupil lacking in self-esteem. The triggers will almost certainly be trivial. Another pupil may be sitting in what this pupil regards as his or her seat. A mild request to pay attention or sit down may provide a flashpoint for loss of temper.

3   **Perfectionism can be a danger sign.** Extreme self-criticism may lead to the constant destruction of work which does not seem to be absolutely perfect. An entire lesson may be taken up with starting and re-starting a piece of work. Other delaying tactics may include fetching or borrowing mainly unnecessary equipment.

4   **Watch how pupils receive praise.** A disconcerting characteristic is the refusal to accept praise, even when it has been well earned. Pupils may respond by criticizing the work, perhaps saying, 'That's rubbish' or by mocking a commendation you may have given for good behaviour. In extreme cases, praise may result in the destruction of a piece of work.

5   **Look out for non-participants.** Refusal to participate in any group or practical activity, even when the other pupils are clearly having fun, is a sign of shaky self-esteem. This pupil may only seem happy in the role of critical spectator. This can lead to unpopularity and isolation, thus confirming a negative self-image.

6   **Be aware of the dangers of sabotage in group situations.** In some cases, such a pupil may be keen to participate in a self-destructive way, acting the part of class clown or deliberately sabotaging the efforts of others, in a possible attempt to halt unwelcome or uncomfortable activities.

7   **Fear of failure may be the motivation for negative reactions to anything new or unexpected.** The introduction of a new subject theme, or a new mode of working, may automatically be met with derision or refusal. For example, the pupil may declare that 'poetry is crap' or 'this is too hard'. A change of teacher may also provoke an uncooperative response.

8   **Dress can give useful clues.** Some pupils may display a negative self-image through their persistent refusal to take off bulky outdoor clothing, or to remove caps or anorak hoods. They hide behind their clothes for protection. They may also carry very large loads of personal belongings from which they refuse to be parted.

9   **Watch for power relationships.** Attempts to buy friendship by the indiscriminate or profligate sharing of sweets or equipment, often with pupils who are powerful members of the group, indicate possible problems with self-esteem. Such offerings may also be given as a result of extortion or bullying.

10   **Look out for signs of escapism.** Pupils with low self-esteem may take refuge in an exciting fantasy life, which they are more likely to share with less apparently sceptical teachers rather than cynical peers. You may be regaled with exciting accounts of meetings with pop stars who just happen to be relatives. Accounts will be given of admiring and attentive boy or girl friends. Alternatively, this pupil may always be about to move to another town or even country. These fantasies provide comfortable illusions for an unhappy pupil.

11

Strategies to improve low self-esteem in pupils

Once you have established that particular pupils think poorly of themselves, you can then look at ways to help them to help themselves. You are unlikely to see miracles overnight, but even tiny steps forward can make a significant difference to often deeply unhappy young people.

1   **Offer praise and encouragement, even for the attainment of very small targets.** Make sure that the pupil understands the progress which is being praised. You could point to an increase in output from the previous lesson, or you could note an improvement in social behaviour.

2   **Use eye contact and appropriate touch when offering praise.** Lightly touch pupils on the hand or shoulder. This helps to tell the pupil that he/she is recognized and valued as an individual. Use pupils' names when addressing them. Other non-verbal contact such as a smile, a thumbs-up sign or a wink can offer reassurance.

3   **Encourage pupils to record their achievements.** This record can then be used to boost confidence when they are too self-critical or defeatist. You can provide a tally card, or a wall chart, to tick targets which have been achieved.

4   **Diffuse anger and reduce negative confrontations.** You can do this by trying more positive responses to unacceptable behaviour. For example, rather than saying, 'You are a lazy, rude person' instead say, 'I'm really disappointed' or, 'I'm very surprised, this just isn't like you'. The behaviour is not condoned, but self-esteem is maintained and another chance is implicitly given.

5   **Listen effectively and actively to your pupils' verbal and non-verbal messages.** Make your body language say you are listening. Lean forward slightly and make eye contact. Don't be afraid to remain silent for longer than is usually comfortable. Signal that you are still listening by saying 'Yes' or 'Hmm!' Nod your head in acknowledgement. These strategies will help the pupil to feel understood. Ask if the pupil would like a further discussion of the problem.

6   **Role play can play a useful part in raising self-esteem.** This can take place within any lesson, not just Drama. If pupils are allowed not to be themselves for a while, they may lose their inhibitions and their fear of failure. Ask the pupil to perform a given task as though they are the most able person in the school, or to give an opinion as though they were the headteacher.

7   **Minimize fear of failure.** Pupils who think of themselves as failures will go to great lengths to avoid situations where failure might occur. You can appear to take the risk for the pupil. For instance, you could say, 'This is very difficult, it's my fault for giving you such hard work, but try your best'. Or you could say, 'Let me try to explain it better'.

8   **Help your pupils to see how good self-esteem develops.** Think of all the things that have enhanced your own positive image of yourself. Perhaps you are an acknowledged great cook or mountain climber. Think about how you became good at it, and how you found out you were. Think about ways to help create an environment whereby your pupil can learn a special skill, or improve upon skills they already possess, and share them with others.

9   **Empathize with your pupil's lack of self-esteem.** Perhaps also share with pupils your own experiences of being unsuccessful, such as failing a driving test or giving up learning to touch type, and talk to your pupil about how that felt for you at the time.

10   **Create special responsibilities.** Place your pupil in a position of responsibility where success is attainable. Small duties, such as collecting the register or acting as book monitor, may pass a positive message that the pupil is trusted and needed.

11   **Show your pupil how to be a friend.** Offer friendship within the boundaries of a teacher/pupil relationship. Whatever your personal style of friendship, you can be there to offer support and offer a role model of how to be a friend.

12

Establishing successful school contact with parents and carers

Parents and carers of pupils with special needs may be your best allies in helping them to make progress, and certainly should be informed and consulted about developments, worries and specific problems. Building these links is an important part of the special needs teacher's role.

1 **Be aware that pupils are cared for in all kinds of different family patterns.** The primary care givers may be birth parents, step parents, grandparents or other relatives, foster parents or foster home care workers. There may be one, two or more people looking after them. The patterns of care may change from time to time as circumstances change.

2 **Be sensitive by not assuming that every pupil has a mum and dad at home.** Pupils are likely be particularly put out if you make sweeping assumptions about who cares for them. Be aware, too, that divorced or separated parents may both wish to be consulted about special needs issues, and may not wish to do so in the same room at the same time. Where records provide separate addresses for parents, it may be necessary to send communications about issues of concern or achievements to both addresses.

3 **Remember that parents and carers are already involved in the education of pupils with special needs.** Be aware that parents and carers are significant partners in the education of pupils with special education needs. Explore ways in which you can establish regular contact. Check the policy of the school and follow procedures carefully. Keep records of all contacts and share these with pastoral staff who may offer advice about effective parental contact.

4   **Plan your appointments with parents or carers.** If you make a formal appointment in school, find a room where you will not be interrupted or overheard. Ensure you have some time alone with them before the pupil's arrival. Take notice of the interaction between parents/carers and pupil. This may provide you with useful clues as to behaviour or give good indications for potential solutions.

5   **Try to keep appointments informal.** Informal meetings with parents/carers can often be extremely effective as they are less stressful for them. For pupils whose parents/carers wish to drop in without appointment, you could establish that you are available for about fifteen minutes after school on a named day of the week.

6   **Remember that meeting parents/carers in school may sometimes present difficulties.** Take good care not to compromise your safety or security. If a parent/carer has a history of difficult behaviour, ask a senior member of staff, say a Head of Year, to be present at your meeting. Make any necessary notes after the meeting. Keep calm and listen carefully. Make sure you say what you need to say. Include the parent/carer in potential solutions.

7   **Be ready to meet parents/carers from a wide range of cultural and linguistic backgrounds.** You may need an interpreter. Try to avoid using your pupil in this role. In respect of behavioural problems, explain the requirements of the school and establish a mutually agreed code of conduct in school. Do not imply any criticism of parental life styles.

8   **Maintain contact efficiently.** Communication with parents/carers can be time consuming if you rely solely on written or telephone contact. A useful way of informal contact is by using a daily notebook carried to lessons by the pupil and shown to parents/carers each night. They may then respond to teachers' comments and send back their own.

9   **Work out how best to respond to truancy.** Responding to truancy is usually the role of the form tutor or other pastoral staff. You may, however, establish a successful daily arrangement, whereby you telephone the parent/carer immediately about any unexplained absence.

10 **Help parents and carers to help their pupils.** They may be willing to help in literacy programmes at home, but may need some help and advice from you before they can cooperate. Can you provide some books or resources for loan? You might suggest a regular 10 minutes per night, rather than an occasional marathon. Shared newspaper reading can be helpful.

11   **Consider letting parents/carers observe in the classroom.** It may be impractical to enlist the help of parents/carers with work in the classroom, but it can be useful in the case of behavioural difficulties if you arrange for them to observe their pupil in class. This may produce a starting point for a cooperative approach to the problem.

12   **Don't base each contact on a problem.** Parents and carers of pupils with special educational needs are used to visiting the school in response to complaints or anxieties. Perhaps you can involve these parents/carers in more enjoyable activities, such as field trips or summer outings. This may be the only opportunity for them to see their pupils in an environment in which they excel.

13

Responding to physical impairment

There may be pupils in your classroom who have a permanent or temporary physical impairment, which may result in mobility problems, difficulties with keeping still or attention problems caused by trying to work while experiencing constant pain. In addition to their educational needs, there may be other needs which you may not previously have encountered. Some of the following ideas may be useful to you.

1   **Relax and be yourself.** Your pupil doesn't need an over anxious teacher, so do not fuss around them, causing them to feel self-conscious and drawing attention to the difficulty. Offer the chance of independence wherever possible and scrupulously avoid patronizing such pupils by doing things for them that they are capable of doing themselves.

2   **Ensure that you know of any potential problems.** Read the Statement of Special Educational Needs carefully and make sure that you understand the implications of the information contained within it.

3   **Be prepared for contingencies.** Find out what to do in an emergency or if any medication might be needed, for example, with asthmatics and diabetics. Liaise with parents and with any specialists in the school, such as a school nurse. Remember that a little knowledge is a dangerous thing, so don't intervene if you don't know what you are doing. Trust the pupil, since people with physical impairments often know a great deal about their own conditions. If you feel disadvantaged by your own lack of knowledge, take a first aid course and seek out specialist advice.

4   **Don't be surprised if your pupil is grumpy, distracted or disaffected.** Allow for fatigue and depression and modify your demands accordingly, but watch out ,too, for clever pupils who can manipulate gullible teachers.

5   **Consider the special needs of pupils with mobility problems.** You may need to rearrange the furniture to accommodate a wheelchair. Plan for this in advance, as pupils may be embarrassed by making a disruptive arrival and having to make everyone else move so they can be accommodated.

6   **Welcome and make use of any additional support your pupil may have.** A wheelchair user may have a carer in the classroom. This person is your best line of communication about the needs of your pupil, so make sure you establish a good working relationship. Extend a warm welcome to your classroom.

7   **Help the pupil with physical impairment to work independently of the carer from time to time.** It can sometimes be hard for an adolescent pupil to accept the presence of a 'minder'. Perhaps you could suggest that the carer works with other pupils or helps with classroom tasks. Everyone may enjoy the break.

8   **Be vigilant to help physically impaired pupils who encounter teasing or bullying.** Obviously you will wish to help but don't over react. A quiet word to the offender may be all that is required. Persistent bullying, however, should be dealt with by senior school staff.

9   **Check in advance how your pupil wishes you to deal with teasing, if this seems appropriate.** It could be a common occurrence, which the pupil may prefer to deal with personally. Some pupils may have developed skills which you don't yet possess. Don't assume that a frail body means a fragile personality, but do not withhold help if you judge that it is needed.

10   **Plan ahead when you know absences will occur.** Frequent absences may impede a pupil's progress. So make plans for known absences and provide work which can be done readily in uncomfortable circumstances, such as hospital wards. You might like to consider encouraging your class to practise their English skills by writing letters to their fellow pupil, to help maintain contact through a long absence.

11   **Remember that pupils who cannot take part in every aspect of school life may suffer from feelings of isolation.** Explore ways for your pupil to develop compensatory skills and focus on any special talents. If there are no obvious areas of excellence, perhaps you can devise some special responsibilities in the classroom. Make sure your pupil is a fully participating member of the group. Remember this may also include being told off when behaving badly.

14

Devising or modifying homework

An important part of helping pupils with special needs to see themselves as part of the regular class is for them to have regular and challenging homework. However, what is set for the whole class may be totally unsuitable for an individual pupil with special needs. Setting tasks that are relevant, stretching and at the right level for the pupil to have a reasonable chance of succeeding is a complex task; these tips are designed to give a few practical pointers on how to achieve this.

1   **Use your time management skills when setting homework for pupils with special needs.** If the task is to be fully understood, it needs to be explained in a calm and unhurried manner. You will need a minimum of ten minutes to do so and, if possible, the work should be given out at the start of the lesson. Write the task clearly on the board. Check that pupils have understood what is required.

2   **The purpose of the homework should be made clear to them.** You can explain how it will help them to understand the lesson better, or prepare them for the next piece of work. Let pupils know if and when the task is to be tested.

3   **Plan ahead for written homework.** Cloze and sequencing tasks are easily devised from the content of the lesson. Make lists of key words for spelling. Vary length and sophistication of response on standard homework tasks.

4   **Pick other people's brains.** It is not necessary to reinvent the wheel. Look at colleagues' resources; the subject matter might not always be appropriate for your purposes, but the methods and strategies may adapt. Book fairs and exhibitions provide masses of ideas and often plenty of free samples if you show interest. Primary school resources may be of

use, but be careful that illustrations are not too young for your pupils. Nevertheless, there is a good chance that you will be able to customize or adapt materials for your target pupils.

5   **Remember that homework tasks need not require a written response.** Drawing and labelling will improve vocabulary and can be used to contribute to classroom display. You can set spellings and tables to be tested later. Pupils can report back orally on findings of set tasks, such as interviewing a grandparent about the war or recounting an item from the previous night's news.

6   **Clarify to pupils that homework does not have to be done at home.** Keep pupils informed about any after school clubs available. Tell pupils if you can offer ten minutes at lunch times to go over what is required. You might also be able to persuade colleagues to share in a cooperative venture to supervise or support homework. It can take some work off your shoulders and the pupils may enjoy a change of company.

7   **Motivate pupils to do homework by showing them that you value it.** Mark and return homework as quickly as possible. Make sure pupils see you recording homework and praise punctual delivery. Spell out your expectations and refuse to settle for less, but make sure your expectations are realistic. Insist on corrections. Keep a regularly changing display of homework on a special board in the classroom. Finally, show your appreciation with suitable awards.

8   **Note that projects need guidelines and regular supervision.** It is all too easy for pupils to be daunted by seemingly huge tasks, or conversely to feel that it can all be done at the last minute. Set short deadlines and small structured tasks. Suggest where the relevant information can be found. Check and store each piece of work as it is completed. Make friends with the school librarian and try to give plenty of notice of imminent projects.

9   **Be aware that homework can aid oral skills too.** You can ask pupils to obtain information which can be delivered orally as a change from having a written task for everything. For example, asking pupils to learn a few lines of a simple poem, or to make up a short dialogue with a partner, can be fun and can add variety to what pupils often see as drudgery.

10   **Remember that reading skills can be developed through homework.** You can have standby reading homework for those occasions when you don't want to set written work. You could suggest that pupils read story books to younger siblings. Find some easy reading texts with more mature story lines. Keep a record of what has been read and encourage pupils to recommend books they have enjoyed to others. Give achievement awards for an agreed number of books read each term.

15

Identifying strengths and weaknesses for multi-sensory teaching strategies

Multi-sensory teaching techniques allow pupils with a range of learning difficulties to access their education in the ways best suited to meet their needs. This means that both their strengths and weaknesses are accounted for. If a pupil has a weakness in one sensory area, then using a strength in another area can help to compensate and encourage the use of strategies to overcome the weakness. Teaching to a weakness through a strength encourages a sense of success and confidence, rather than reinforcing failure.

1   **When teaching a new concept in your subject, be aware of the pupil's strengths and weaknesses.** Use the strength first to motivate the pupil into success. If you then follow up with a series of exercises that simultaneously input the information through as many senses as possible (seeing, hearing, saying, feeling), then the memory can store this information more effectively and give the weak sense some back-up material to aid recall.

2   **Use a series of activities for assessing strengths and weaknesses that can prove to be fun for both you and the pupil.** You may prefer to do this with the pupil on their own or make it part of a small-group activity. It could be difficult for you to do these in a large class and to be able to note down the results. You will need to have prepared materials in advance and have a sheet prepared for the results.

3   **Look for ways to expand digit span recall.** This is the amount of information a pupil can handle effectively at any one moment, for example, how many digits in a telephone number can be remembered in order, or

how many letters in a word can be learnt in order. An individual's capacity to recall digits varies, but if it is as low as three or four, then that pupil may have difficulty copying from the board or writing from dictation. You can teach them ways to extend their recall, but you need to know whether they have more difficulty with visual recall or auditory recall.

4   **Test out auditory and visual digit span.** You can do this by preparing a pack of cards with letters or numbers on. The first cards should start with three digits, then move to cards with four digits and so on, until you have cards with eight, nine or more digits. If you think about it, a telephone number has six or seven digits, but if you include the code it can have at least four more.

5   **For visual digit span, show the cards to the pupil one at a time.** Start with the lowest number of digits, and show it for eight seconds. Do not allow any verbal back-up. After eight seconds, turn the card over and ask them to write down what they saw. Repeat this, moving up in numbers of digits. Try to do about three at each level. Make a note of which letters/ numbers they recall correctly, which are recalled out of order and which are totally incorrect. Stop when the pupil has reached their limit, for example, when the pupil is unable to recall most of the correct digits.

6   **For auditory digit span use a similar set of cards but with different digits.** This time you should read the digits to the pupil in a measured voice, taking care not to group the digits. Afterwards you should ask the pupil to repeat the digits back to you. For a variation, you could ask them to write them down. Again, you should make a note of the responses and the limit the pupil reached.

7   **Test for lateral preference.** There are activities you can carry out with the pupil that will help you to decide whether the pupil has a preference as to which hand, foot, eye and ear they use. So a person can be right dominant, that is, always use right hand, foot, eye and ear, or they could have a mixed dominance, where neither right nor left is the sole preference. Similarly, they could have a confused dominance; right dominance in all but one area, where the dominance shifts to left.

8   **Evaluate directionality.** This refers to a pupil's understanding of up/ down, top/bottom, back/front, over/under, inside/outside, as well as left/right. This can be a problem if they have poor awareness of these concepts and find it hard to apply them to instructions. You may find this displays itself in mirror writing or reversals of the letters 'b' and 'd'. You can help this pupil by identifying this, and find ways of strengthening their auditory or visual sequencing memory.

9   **Use a range of activities that help identify these factors.** These could include asking a pupil to write, throw a ball, remove and replace a screw-top lid, hop on one foot, kick a ball, look through a telescope, look through a key hole, listen to a watch, listen at a door and so on. With each activity (at least two for each part of the body), note whether the pupil had a left or right preference. A simple exercise in paper folding (origami) can identify directionality.

10   **Use sequencing activities to identify areas of strength or weakness for multi-sensory teaching.** You could ask the pupil to recite the alphabet, forwards and backwards, days of the week and months of the year. Similarly you could get them to count to twenty singly, then go up in twos, and so on, and go back in reverse.

16

Multi-sensory teaching strategies for specific learning difficulties

Once you have identified the areas of strength and weakness for a pupil, you can begin to devise a series of teaching strategies that may help them with reading, writing, spelling or Specific Learning Difficulty. Multi-sensory methods mean the simultaneous use of the ears, eyes, speech, fingers and muscles. For many people this comes naturally and instinctively, but pupils with Specific Learning Difficulties (SpLD) need to be taught how to use these skills together.

1   **Use the 'Look, Say and Write' approach.** A new word to be learnt is shown and the pupil writes over the word at the board, on the paper and repeats the sound at the same time. You can build more activities into this at the board. You will be surprised how much pupils enjoy coming to the board.

2   **Facilitate independent learning approaches.** Tape recorded work alongside visual display, as in the Language Master machines, can help to reinforce this approach without you needing to work one-to-one with the pupils. Try to ensure that the system you use has a self-correcting facility. You may find the pupil wants to make their own materials; let them, this will motivate them.

3   **Make use of packs of cards with letter patterns printed on one side and words containing them on the reverse.** The pupil looks at the letter pattern and it acts as a cue to remind them of words with that pattern. They say the sound of the letter pattern, for example, 'ai' says 'A', then they recall the clue word on the back of the card (train). At this stage they can turn the card over and see if they were correct.

4   **Use packs of cards like this repeatedly to strengthen the pupil's visual and auditory memory.** They can also help pupils to respond automatically to visual or auditory prompts in the future. You could help by making this a regular starting exercise in a lesson. You could work on a pack of five cards per week.

5   **Use Pelmanism to reinforce learning.** This is a card game that uses the same approach. You might know this game simply as Pairs, where you have to pair up matching cards. You could develop games from this theme, so that the pupil had to find a card with the letter pattern on it that matched the card with the picture of a word spelt with that pattern, and so on.

6   **Use multisensory approaches to bring home the message.** Lesson activities can be planned to ensure that the new work is presented visually on the board, through an experiment/demonstration or video, and then reinforced aurally or orally through written work, a quiz, a tape recording, reading exercise. Wherever possible, try to help pupils experience participation in the presentation of the work, for example, coming to the board, being involved in the demonstration, or giving a talk about an aspect of it. All of these will help to store the information more effectively in the memory.

7   **Don't overlook kinaesthetic memory.** This is the area of the senses where the pupil remembers, through the movement and actions of the body, what has been taught. If you can involve the pupil in some area of activity that is kinaesthetic, it will help them all the more. Try to visualize this area of their learning as 'hands on' experience, such as learning to drive a car and knowing which pedal is which without looking.

8   **Incorporate 'thinking skills' lessons.** Some schools have introduced thinking skills lessons to help pupils to understand which skills they can use across the curriculum and how to maximize on their own strengths. You may have already used the games and activities where you try to extend a pupil's retention of a list as in the 'shopping list' game. Each pupil has to recite the shopping list as far as it has got and then add on one more item. You can have a shopping list the size of a class. Pupils should be taught how to improve their memory by repeating the list in their head, grouping items together, using link ideas and so on.

9   **Train and encourage development in observation skills.** You can play games that teach this skill, such as 'Kim's game', where you show a tray of items and then remove one; pupils have to spot which item was removed. They can do this visually and orally, or they can write down what they saw as a competition.

10   **Give feedback to pupils.** However you approach multi-sensory teaching, you should constantly be giving feedback to the pupil and listening to their feedback. If you have tested their digit span recall and they were weak at recalling what they saw, then suggest to them that they say the digits in their head and keep repeating them until they are asked to write them down. They might find it easy to make up a word from the sound of the digits in order, or to group the digits into pairs or threes. You probably do this to recall telephone numbers.

17

Looking after your needs as a teacher of pupils with special educational needs

Teaching is a stressful job, and working with pupils with special educational needs can be enormously demanding, frustrating and exhausting (as well as being rewarding and satisfying). If you are to be effective in your work, however, you need to ensure that your own needs are catered for, hence the tips in the last part of this section.

1   **Try to make time to work with pupils who do not have special educational needs.** This will ensure that you do not lose sight of the norm or lower your expectations of pupils. You could also offer extension work for more able pupils for use in class, or at lunch times or after school.

2   **Try not to lose touch with your subject.** You will very likely have a subject specialism which you pursued before your entry into this field. On a practical level you may have to support pupils taking examinations and you will need to be aware of curriculum developments. You could also explore the possibility of teaching your subject to adults in your spare time. This may also be a means of keeping your sanity.

3   **Watch your stress levels.** If you are fortunate enough to have a say in your timetable, you can reduce a certain amount of stress by ensuring that the most taxing areas of your work are relieved, or at least sandwiched between the less demanding parts of the week. Try to spread your contact with pupils evenly and in small periods of time to avoid exhaustion and over-exposure.

4   **Have fun with your pupils whenever you can.** Learn to take pleasure in the smallest of their achievements. You can play on-going games, such as the vocabulary game in which you challenge pupils to find words in the dictionary that you cannot explain or spell. You will soon become familiar with the likes of xylophone and zenana. Give small rewards when they catch you out. Challenge them to join you in this game.

5   **Ensure that you avoid frustration at your pupil's rate of progress by being realistic about what they can achieve.** Do not necessarily lower your expectations but be prepared for progress measured in small steps. You may have to wait until someone else notices an improvement. Do not underestimate your part in your pupil's progress.

6   **Don't be afraid to seek help.** Ask for help from other colleagues when you have a pupil who fails to respond to your efforts or resists any attempts to establish a relationship. They may have insights to offer as to what works best with this pupil, or they may reassure you that they have experienced similar difficulties.

7   **Look beyond the school when necessary.** Seek advice from outside agencies if you encounter problems which fail to respond to tried and trusted strategies. Your pupil may previously have had support from educational psychologists who are in regular contact with the school, and who may be prepared to offer advice or information which does not breach confidentiality.

8   **Keep yourself fit.** Make time in your private life for stress-relieving activities such as swimming, dancing, sketching or boat-building, where the tensions of working life are not allowed to intrude. Establish an exclusion zone for yourself. It doesn't mean you don't care, and it will allow time for you to recover and be of more use to your pupils.

9   **Exercise good time management of your free time in school.** Assess very carefully how much time you can spare for lunch time or after school activities. Stick to what you know you can manage. Make it clear when you are not available. You might consider locking the door while you are eating your lunch, if you are subject to interruptions.

10 **Keep an eye on your own physical and emotional health.** Take regular, short breaks. Holidays do not have to be expensive to be effective. If you fail to look after yourself, you cannot hope to be of use to your pupils.

Chapter 2   Improving unacceptable behaviour

This chapter contains a variety of tips to help pupils whose behaviour in the classroom is proving unacceptable. All too often pupils with special needs are assumed to have problematic behaviour simply because their needs are different, and this is not automatically the case. However, some forms of special needs tend to be linked with behavioural problems, and this chapter offers suggestions on how these can best be managed.

18

Devising and evaluating a diagnostic behaviour questionnaire

Sometimes, we are so busy as teachers dealing with the day-to-day business of our work that we don't always effectively record information about pupils that can be helpful to our working practices. Instruments that enable teachers to track and monitor behaviour can be useful in helping to recognize and plan to remediate specific problems that arise. The following set of tips provides guidance on how to devise and evaluate such a tool.

1   **Identify pupils who need your attention.** You may have a special responsibility for a pupil whose behaviour is giving concern in many areas of the school. First, you need to find out, by use of a questionnaire, if this behaviour is common to every situation.

2   **Ensure that your questionnaire is user-friendly.** It should be possible for it to be completed with the minimum of effort. Keep the size to a single A4 page. Word the questions clearly and leave adequate space for replies.

3   **Summarize your concern.** Write a short introductory paragraph of no more than six lines explaining that concern has been expressed about the pupil's behaviour in a number of situations. Make it clear that the questionnaire has been designed to give a quick and comprehensive picture of the pupil's overall behaviour.

4   **Justify your questionnaire.** Emphasize that the aim of the questionnaire is to gain information, which will enable you to work out strategies to help change unacceptable behaviour in lessons where there is a problem.

5   **Assure teachers that the information received will be confidential.** Inexperienced teachers may be nervous about admitting to problems in class. Express appreciation for any answers whatever the opinion expressed. Do not leave the questionnaires in pigeon holes. See each teacher individually and give examples of the sorts of information which will be useful. You may gain insights from this conversation, too.

6   **Your first question should ask for brief details about what exactly causes concern.** Answers in note form will be quite adequate. So often teachers will make vague and unspecified complaints. You need to know whether the problem is, for example, calling out in class or provoking other pupils. Ask for any details of unacceptable behaviour.

7   **Seek out the causes of behaviours.** In order to understand the causes of poor behaviour, it is useful to have some idea of what triggers that behaviour. Your next question could be a consideration of precipitating factors. You could also ask if the teacher is aware of the prevailing conditions when it does *not* occur. This may be just as revealing. For example, it may be the crucial absence of another pupil, the subject or just the time of day.

8   **Think about effects on other pupils.** Your pupil may be causing the most concern in classrooms, but there will very probably be significant interactions with other pupils. Ask for the names of other pupils who are likely to be involved. You could also ask what those pupils are likely to gain from that involvement. Ask if patterns of response have been established, and if they need to be changed to assist your pupil to improve.

9   **Find out what the pupil seems to gain from bad behaviour.** Is it to receive attention or to conceal learning difficulties? Does the pupil seek to enhance self-esteem by gaining the apparent attention of laughing classmates? You can ask your respondent to give an opinion on the outcome for the pupil of this behaviour.

10 **Probe into what has succeeded, and what has not.** The final question, which you can ask before you begin to devise your own strategies for improvement, is about which strategies have worked for this teacher and, equally importantly, which ones have failed. Provide some space for any other relevant information. You can then use the results of your questionnaire to help you to plan your own action.

19

Strategies to cope with rude and negative behaviour

Unpleasant behaviour can be difficult to cope with, and even though we know there are often good reasons for pupils' rudeness and negativity, we can all do with a helping hand sometimes. These tips are designed to offer a range of approaches, with some suggestions on how to react in these circumstances.

1   **Refuse to take the blame for rudeness.** Remember, the anger that is directed at you may spring from a variety of problems over which you have no control. Try not to bear grudges, however hurt you are. Start every day afresh with high expectations of pupil behaviour.

2   **Avoid losing your own temper, even though you may have been badly provoked.** Remember, you are the adult and you have a responsibility to provide a good role model. Ensure that you do not raise your voice more than is strictly necessary. Noisy and volatile behaviour from you will be mirrored in your pupils' response.

3   **Try to use humour to diffuse tension.** If you give an angry pupil the opportunity to back off without losing face, you may prevent an unpleasant incident. For example, if a pupil shouts, 'I hate you', you could perhaps smile and say, 'That's a shame, because I like you'. Be careful, however, not to make the pupil the object of derisory laughter from the rest of the class. The goal is to diffuse tension, not to create it.

4   **Mirror the behaviour of the pupil.** If a pupil has been offensive or aggressive, you could say, 'Have I ever been anything but courteous and supportive to you?' This clearly presupposes that this is true. If you cannot in all conscience put such a question, then you could ask the pupil which is preferable – a patient teacher who makes polite requests or one who storms and shouts. If that is what the pupil agrees is more desirable, then it makes a good point.

5   **Try to establish a minimum set of rules of behaviour.** Make sure that these rules are applied consistently and fairly. Very often bad behaviour is the result of pupils not knowing where boundaries lie. Your pupils must be absolutely clear about which offence will result in which sanction. The probable inconsistencies in their own lives should not be reproduced in the classroom. Firmness and consistency create stability.

6   **Make any punishments positive.** When your pupil has accepted that the behaviour must be punished in some way, you could ask the pupil to suggest an appropriate punishment. It may be that the suggestion is too severe and you can settle for something less strict. Another way of punishing is to use a 'symbolic punishment', which can be written on a piece of paper and thrown away if agreed conditions, such as clearing up mess or apologizing, are met by the end of the lesson.

7   **Make use of cooling off procedures (and this includes you).** You may be able to place the pupil in the corridor for a brief period, although many schools now discourage this for obvious reasons. It may be possible for you to ask a nearby colleague to accommodate your pupil for a few minutes. You may judge it sensible to leave the room yourself on some pretext, which gives the pupil time to calm down. However, do not leave pupils in a situation that could prove dangerous.

8   **Try to enable your pupil to empathize with your feelings.** When pupils are rude, we often respond with a warning message such as, 'Sit down', 'Shut up' or, 'You are always starting trouble'. The message implies that the pupil is the problem. You could try letting the pupil know how you feel. Explain instead of blaming. For example, you could say, 'If you talk to Malik when I am reading this story, I get really frustrated and it stops me from finishing the story'. This places your distress on the effect of the behaviour, not on the pupil.

9   **Find ways of making encouraging statements which the pupil can accept without feeling patronized.** Offer praise for the smallest of advances such as, 'I noticed that you kept your temper when Tara took your rubber without asking. Well done'. You can find other ways of making positive statements such as complimenting a pupil on sporting achievements.

10   **Agree contracts for improving negative behaviour.** You could suggest target weeks for focusing on one particular problem, such as not swearing or shouting at other pupils or the teacher. Perhaps you could enlist the support of parents and ask them to look at the comments on the target sheet. Make sure that improvements are noticed and rewarded.

20

Dealing with pupils whose emotional and behavioural difficulties lead to disaffection and isolation in the classroom

These pupils form a disparate group, ranging from social isolates to school refusers. They are not likely to give much trouble in the classroom, but they are probably giving anxiety elsewhere about their lack of educational and social progress.

1   **Identify pupils in this category.** Make sure you know as much as possible about them and consult Individual Education Plans. Refer any pupils you are concerned about to the SENCO or Head of Year to make sure their special needs are picked up.

2   **Record and report absences.** Poor attendance is a useful indication of disaffection, but it is easy to lose track without good record-keeping. Be welcoming when your pupils do appear, and try not to overload pupils with missed work or issue pessimistic predictions about potential failure.

3   **Place pupils on internal attendance report.** Selective attendance is a familiar feature of this problem, so you need to make sure you have the necessary data to help you spot patterns.

4   **Seat your disaffected pupil in a sympathetic group.** You can also ensure that regular group activities take place and encourage this pupil to take some part in activities which feel comfortable and non-threatening.

5   Check to see if there are any practical reasons for this pupil's isolation. For example, a pupil may have some unpleasant habits or an unacceptable level of body odour. You can either engage in some diplomatic counselling yourself, or you could refer the pupil to the school nurse or to pastoral staff for extra help. You can also contact parents for their support, although you may find that home is the root of the problem.

6   Be aware that depressed or disaffected pupils may be victims of sexual abuse. If you have any anxieties or suspicions, report them to the designated key teacher for sexual abuse in your school. You can also say to the pupil that you have noticed that they are worried and offer to listen or guide them towards a more appropriately qualified colleague.

7   Check to see if your pupil is being bullied. Victims of bullying can retreat into silence and suffer alone. If you don't feel you know the best way to deal with this matter yourself, refer the pupil to pastoral staff. If your school has any special anti-bullying strategies, you can refer your pupil to the people responsible for their implementation.

8   Keep yourself informed about the intervention of any outside agencies by reference to the SENCO or pastoral staff. It could be that a disaffected pupil may be receiving psychiatric help. This can lead to a deterioration in behaviour in the initial stages which, if you know about it, will make it easier to understand and accommodate adverse changes in behaviour. You may also be able to gain information about which classes are likely to be missed because of external appointments.

9   Try to enthuse bright pupils who are underachieving because of personal problems. You can provide stimulating work at a challenging level (not just another worksheet!). Perhaps you can involve this pupil in helping less able pupils from time to time. It may also be possible to create occasional groups of high-flyers to meet from other classes at certain times to work on special projects to provide an effective and challenging peer group.

10 Be aware that you may possibly have a pupil who has been traumatized. For example, pupils who are refugees may have undergone appalling personal experiences, such as war or murder. This pupil may be withdrawn and over-sensitive to noise, arguments or teasing or, on the other hand, the reaction may be one of frenetic and anti-social behaviour. Try to place the pupil in a supportive group with pupils who speak the same language, if this is appropriate. Offer your own personal support by lending a sympathetic ear, or providing shelter from the boisterous school environment at breaks and lunch times.

21

Assisting the reintegration of excluded pupils

When pupils have been excluded, the process of re-entry can often be a difficult and painful affair. As a special needs teacher, you may have a good relationship with such a pupil and any advice you can offer may prove invaluable. The tips that follow aim to enable you to build bridges and assist reintegration.

1   **Act as a broker to facilitate reintegration.** An ideal way to facilitate the prodigal's return would be to arrange meetings with class teachers in advance to restore working relations and to spell out ground rules without the presence of fellow pupils, although in many cases this will not be possible.

2   **Manage the occasion of first reappearance.** One suggestion you could make is that the pupil should arrive at this first crucial lesson in plenty of time, preferably without a cohort of encouraging acolytes and certainly avoiding any display of defiance or disaffection.

3   **Do all you can to make resumption of study a trouble free process.** It would be helpful if you could arrange to be available to this pupil on a daily basis at the start of the day to provide practical help. Check if the pupil is adequately equipped for lessons and have some pens to lend if necessary. It is also a good opportunity to discuss potential difficulties and to prepare some coping strategies.

4   **Try to make sure that any necessary paperwork is handled with minimum fuss.** Advise your pupil to present any authorisation to return, or any report card, immediately on arrival and without being asked. If the teacher is busy, these can be slipped unobtrusively on the desk.

5   **Advise returning pupils about how to interact with classmates.** Those returning after exclusion should be made aware of the pitfalls which 'best friends' may present to a smooth return. They may be expecting a return of the entertaining behaviour which led to exclusion. Suggest that your pupil prepares some face saving excuses as to why trouble must be avoided or seating reallocated. An example might be, 'My dad will kill me/ground me'.

6   **Brief your fellow teachers about how to help the returner to reintegrate.** The welcome back by other teachers may be unfriendly and this could cause further problems, especially if the first words that greet the returner hark back to the original cause of exclusion.

7   **Remind the returner that teachers have bad days too.** Prepare for this eventuality by rehearsing a low key response for the pupil to use in these circumstances. Help your pupil to realize that a place back in the group will have to be earned.

8   **Help them to find the words they need to get them out of trouble.** If your pupil misses vital working instructions at the start of the lesson, suggest a conciliatory approach such as, 'I haven't quite understood all of that, would you mind saying it again, please'.

9   **Find ways to inform fellow teachers of your pupil's good intentions.** Encourage comments from them to you at daily briefings about the returner's progress and devise trouble free ways for teachers to let you know of improvements or difficulties.

10   **Share this feedback with the pupil, parents and pastoral staff.** Use any available opportunities to engage your pupil in some self-assessment in order to raise awareness of existing problems. The more pupils are able to understand what is going on, the more likely it is that they will be able to take some responsibility for their own actions.

11   **Don't allow a breakdown of the reintegration to dishearten you too much.** If, after all your work, comes the final and perhaps inevitable exclusion, remember that some of your efforts may bear fruit in another place at another time. Education, like politics, is the art of the possible.

22

Supporting pupils who are being bullied

Bullying is widespread and can have really serious long-term outcomes as has been highlighted recently in the media. Teachers have a responsibility to ensure that pupils are kept safe in schools and that this repugnant behaviour is not tolerated. However, this is far from an easy task, and these tips do not pretend to provide foolproof strategies to stamp it out. However, teachers might find some of the suggestions useful in supporting pupils who are experiencing bullying.

1   **Discuss the problem with the class.** It is not necessary to be specific about individual cases or names. You can perhaps say that some pupils in the class are being bullied. You could then organize discussions on how to deal with bullying.

2   **Establish firm rules for classroom behaviour.** Involve the class in making these rules. Reassure pupils that telling about bullying isn't 'telling tales' or 'grassing'. All pupils have the right to be safe from bullying, and the consequences of ignoring it can be very serious.

3   **Recognize and deal with negative group dynamics.** Assign safe places for vulnerable pupils, but make sure that this does not lead to isolation. Place bullies next to strong and confident pupils. Break up any groups which threaten the atmosphere of the class. Assist peer group pressure against bullies and help coerced members of bullying groups to extricate themselves from that situation.

4   **Teach your pupils some self-assertiveness strategies to cope with bullying.** Reassure bullied pupils that it is not their fault. Show pupils how to adopt a confident body posture and how to maintain steady eye contact. You can also provide pupils with some ready responses to deal

with taunts and insults. They don't have to be brilliantly witty, but victims often say it helps to be prepared. Suggest something like, 'That's what you think', instead of looking hurt and upset.

5   **Encourage pupils to seek help against bullying.** A simple and private way of enabling pupils to ask for help is to provide a bully box (to which only you have access), where they can drop notes about their worries and concerns. Follow up all complaints quickly and involve all pupils concerned.

6   **Protect and shelter exceptionally vulnerable pupils at certain points in the day.** Involve senior staff in any decisions about leaving classes early. You may be able to provide a listening post at certain times for pupils who are suffering badly. You may, perhaps, also wish to contact parents to discuss strategies for helping their pupils to cope.

7   **Enable pupils to help and protect themselves.** Suggest that pupils tell a friend what is happening and ask him/her for support. Encourage pupils to conceal their distress or anger from the bully. Explain that the bully gets pleasure from such a reaction. Discourage pupils from hitting back, by explaining that this may be dangerous or that they may even be blamed for starting the trouble. You could also suggest that one way of taking the wind out of the sails of a bully is to ask for the remark to be repeated. It also gives an element of control to the victim.

8   **Build up the self-esteem of bullied pupils.** Suggest that pupils make a list of all the good things about themselves, and urge them to record whenever other people say positive things about them. You could suggest that pupils extend their range of activities, which might increase self-confidence, such as classes in self-defence, trampolining or getting a Saturday job.

9   **Every school should have an anti-bullying policy in place.** Check that you know the details of your school's policy. If there does not seem to be a written policy, perhaps you can request a staff meeting to discuss this omission.

10   **Make use of professional expertise to combat bullying.** *Kidscape* is a registered charity which provides free booklets for pupils, parents and schools. In addition, they produce a great many resources for use in school as well as providing in-school programmes. They also provide legal advice and helplines for pupils and parents. Details on how to contact *Kidscape* are provided in the Information Section at the end of this book.

23

Helping bullies to change their behaviour

It may seem strange to suggest that bullies have special needs, but if we want to stamp out bullying, we may need from time to time to tackle the problem at source, and that means working with the pupils who are themselves bullies. If we can get them to change their behaviour, it will make our lives easier and will help both the bullies and the pupils who are their victims.

1 **Establish the causes and circumstances of bullying.** You can try to find out if pupils have some understanding of why they bully. Sometimes temporary bullying is the result of trauma, such as divorce or bereavement. If the pupil cannot or will not offer an explanation, check with pastoral staff or special needs staff for any relevant information.

2 **Keep accurate records of incidents.** You can easily devise a standard form which is quickly filled in with details of each incident. Interview bullies and victims and obtain written statements from all parties. Record the penalties and outcome. These notes may be useful as a record of deteriorating or improving behaviour, or to help parents accept unpalatable truths about their pupils.

3 **Raise the self-awareness of the bullying pupils.** Such pupils may offer a variety of false excuses, such as 'It was just a laugh', 'It was an accident', 'He started it by picking on me'. You could try to get pupils to face up to the fact that very few people were laughing, or that no one shared the view that it was an accident or provocation.

4 **Try to improve bullying pupils' self-esteem.** Reassure pupils that, although their behaviour is unacceptable, they are still valued. It is the behaviour which is not liked, not them. Bullies are often as unhappy as their victims and equally in need of help. Offer assistance to help change behaviour.

5   **Set firm guidelines for future behaviour.** You could make it clear what the punishment will be for bullying behaviour. You can also suggest ways in which pupils can make amends to their victims. Prepare them for the possibility that it may take some time for them to be trusted and help them to keep on trying. Give recognition and rewards for improved behaviour. Praise publicly, if this seems appropriate.

6   **Identify situations which lead to bullying.** Try to find out which lessons or teachers make the pupil misbehave. It might be useful to explore what the bullying pupil is likely to gain from this behaviour, even if it is a negative gain, such as being sent out of a lesson and avoiding a difficult task.

7   **Devise strategies to help pupils control aggressive behaviour.** You could suggest that pupils set personal goals, such as, 'I won't bug Mark today' or, 'I'll try not to wind up Sita when I see her at lunch'. You could try to get pupils to recognize danger signs and have strategies in place to cope. For instance, old tricks such as holding your breath and counting to ten can still be effective.

8   **Control your own reactions to bullying behaviour.** Although you will wish to respond firmly and swiftly, avoid showing anger or disgust. Try to keep calm while putting an end to the incident. You could perhaps have a 'time out' seat in the corridor or at the front of your desk, where the pupil can sit until calm is restored. It might help you, too. Give praise and encouragement if the pupil can apologize.

9   **Enlist parental cooperation.** Check first with pastoral staff to see if this will be appropriate. Be prepared for parents to be distressed and possibly disbelieving. Put them fully in the picture with your records of incidents. Try to be reassuring and positive about their pupil, and suggest solutions to which you can all contribute.

10   **Recommend the resources of professional organizations to help bullies and their families.** *Kidscape* (see Information Section) produce free leaflets and advice for pupils who wish to stop bullying. There are also counselling services and helplines available to help both bullies and their victims.

24

Improving the ethos of a problem class

Sometimes it seems as if a whole class has become a problem, and it is often difficult to know how best to tackle the problem without tarring the whole group with the same brush, or setting up for yourself expectations of how they will behave without this becoming a self-fulfilling prophesy. These tips aim to help you get to the centre of the issues by looking at ways to improve the ethos of the class as a whole.

1 **Identify the root of the problem.** Is the class unrelentingly difficult, or are some subject areas trouble free? Find out if the removal of one or two crucial members would benefit the class. Is there an imbalance of gender or ability? Are there more pupils with behavioural difficulties than in similar groups? Have they suffered from changes of staff?

2 **Do not attempt to go it alone.** Seek the support of pastoral staff and colleagues who also teach this class. Try to agree on a whole-school approach to the problem. Stick to what has been agreed and let pupils know this is a concerted effort.

3 **Institute a range of strategies to improve behaviour.** You may need the presence of a senior member of staff to help you get this off to a good start. You could follow simple rules, such as getting the pupils to line up quietly outside the room before entering, or to follow your seating plan without question. There are very many different kinds of strategies you can follow, but the main thing is not to relax your efforts and to be consistent in their application.

4   **Maintain the momentum of a new start.** Don't become complacent when things get better, as they can soon slip back again. However, be generous with your recognition of any improvements. If you have to point out bad behaviour, show pupils how hurt and disappointed you are and avoid shouting and complaining. Encourage them to try again and express your support for them.

5   **Devise positive sanctions and punishments.** Try not to impose whole-class punishments. There are always some pupils who have not misbehaved and they may be crucial allies for you in your plan for improvement. You could try, perhaps, to draw up a rota for tidying up after each lesson. This might avoid the necessity for keeping everyone in to clear up a ravaged classroom. You could apply this to a wide range of tasks.

6   **Reward all improvements consistently.** At first you may only be praising the first ten minutes of a lesson, or the fact that no one started a fight or arrived late to the lesson. Set long term targets with rewards, such as trips out of school at the end of term or a free choice of activity in a lesson. Involve the class in self-assessment, if possible.

7   **Bring in reinforcements if necessary.** There will be times when you just cannot manage the problem alone. Perhaps the form tutor could be asked to cooperate on the issue of class behaviour during tutorial periods. You could ask the Head of Year, or a senior member of staff, to drop in 'unexpectedly' on your lessons. This can work for praise as well as censure.

8   **Be aware of the needs of your well-behaved pupils.** They are bound to be suffering from the disruptive behaviour of their classmates. Assure them of your understanding of the problem, and let them know what you are trying to do to solve it. Try not to create divisions in the group by holding up your 'good' pupils as examples to your 'bad' ones. Let their positive behaviour contribute to an unspoken class ethos.

9   **Monitor and assess improvement on a regular basis.** Keep detailed running records of behaviour, attendance and punctuality. Make pupils aware of changes and improvements, which you or other members of staff have noticed and reward and praise generously. Show the class you are proud of them whenever possible.

10 **Be realistic about the rate of improvement.** Try not to get downhearted if the class seems to take one step forward and six back. You cannot change behavioural problems overnight, and sometimes you may be too close to see changes that others have begun to appreciate.

25

Dealing with disruption in the classroom

If you are to provide effective help for pupils who are disruptive, it is essential that you win some early battles. At first you may need to enlist additional support, but in the long run it is all up to you. The following suggestions may help you to nip problems in the bud and establish a pleasant and calm environment in your classroom.

1   **Make it quite clear that choice of seating is non-negotiable.** Quickly establish that the pupil must sit where directed without argument or pleading. Allowing the disruptive pupil to sit in the middle of a bunch of mates, in an area where it is difficult for the teacher to monitor, is asking for trouble.

2   **Deal with late arrivals quickly and with minimal fuss.** Lateness to lessons provides great potential for disruption. If you are already speaking to the class, motion the pupil to stand at your desk until you are free. Record lateness and deal with that later.

3   **Set out achievable targets for pupils with special needs at every lesson.** One target could be that the pupil enters the room quietly and sits where directed. Another might be that the pupil does not call out across the room to others.

4   **Ensure that improvements do not go unnoticed.** Give praise for the smallest achievement and devise a simple form to record accumulated points. This will help the pupil to see that even tiny advances are acknowledged.

5   **Keep your cool when things start to get out of hand.** Troubled pupils often over-react to normal classroom situations. There will be raised voices and arguments. Don't be tempted to join in. Keep calm at all times. Lower your voice while keeping reassuring eye contact. Provide a positive role model for your pupil.

6   **Reinforce your calm image by your body language.** Try to relax. Don't look worried or cross. Don't wave your arms about or make sudden jerky movements. You may find it difficult to do so when chaos seems to be breaking out, but it might be the case that your tranquillity is catching.

7   **Find out what you can about the background of your disruptive pupil.** Knowing what is causing your pupil's problems will help you to deal with the consequences. Consult all available records and talk to SENCOs and pastoral staff about how best to help in the classroom.

8   **Keep in touch with parents and carers wherever possible.** Positive contact with home can be a crucial area of support. For some pupils a daily notebook, in which you can record brief comments and provide space for parental response, is helpful. However, you may judge that this is not as beneficial as referral to a trusted Head of Year, SENCO or other key teacher.

9   **Make use of other pupils in the classroom to help your pupil to settle back into work.** Positive peer group pressure can be used to good effect. However, be aware of the dangers of scapegoating and paying back old scores. Try to enlist the help of pupils you can trust to encourage and befriend your troubled pupil.

10   **Try not to take anger personally.** You will often be the target of a great deal of anger from a pupil with emotional and behavioural problems. It is not really meant for you. Start every day afresh and do not bear grudges. Learn to like your troubled pupils. Remember, the pleasant young adult you bump into in five year's time might be the pupil who gave you the most sleepless nights. It can be reassuring then to think that perhaps you were part of the solution after all.

Chapter 3   Specific special needs issues

This chapter contains tips on a range of specific special needs that you may encounter in your classroom. Obviously the scope of this book makes it impossible to deal with any of these issues in great detail, but we aim to provide some practical pointers on how to identify particular special needs and some steps you can take to give your pupils with these special needs the best possible chance to thrive in your classes.

26

Identifying and meeting the needs of able/gifted pupils

A pupil who has learning or behavioural difficulties and has problems accessing their education fully in school is probably what most people think of when they hear the term Special Needs. However, it is equally true that an able pupil, whose potential is either not recognized or developed, also has special needs in relation to their education. In some schools, you will find that the same department is responsible both for ensuring that such pupils are identified and have their needs met, and for the special needs of pupils who have learning or behavioural difficulties. The following tips are designed to clarify whether a child requires provision in this area and how it might best be achieved.

1 **Find out whether the school has an Able Pupils' Policy.** More than this, do different departments have local policies? If these documents exist, look to see how the term *able* or *gifted* is defined for all concerned; you cannot work within a policy until you know what its criteria are.

2 **Aim to discover how the policies are implemented.** Look to see if there is a whole school approach, or whether individual departments have their own system of identification, intervention and extension work. Some schools operate 'fast tracking' classes, where the pupils take examinations a year early or are placed on a more advanced examination syllabus. You may find that the school has extension classes after school or can arrange for this pupil to attend 'master classes'.

3 **Clarify the terminology.** Agreement on what is meant by able or gifted varies. You might find that the school or authority have defined the most able or gifted as that top 2% of the school population who are exceptionally talented. This is comparable with the 2% at the lower end (Statemented pupils), who have extreme learning difficulties. Similarly, you may find that there are 18% of pupils just above and below these 2% who have special needs; this 18% of gifted pupils may drift in and out of 'gifted' phases.

4   **Remember that giftedness may be apparent in a range of areas.** It is certainly not just limited to high IQ. A pupil may display exceptional talent in any of the following areas: physical ability; artistic ability; mechanical ingenuity; leadership; high intelligence; creativity.

5   **Be aware that identification can be difficult as criteria are hard to agree on.** You might find that the pupil can be identified by teachers or as the result of tests. An educational psychology assessment may highlight the talent or the school may have its own set of checklists. It may be that you, or the pupil, have a general awareness of an innate talent and that there is much more to offer. Sometimes the provision already in place for a pupil can reveal that they are finding it too easy and insufficiently challenging.

6   **Watch out for stereotyping.** You may have a stereotyped image of an able pupil as one who is a 'bookworm' or has a high IQ. If you are not careful, this can act as a barrier to recognizing and developing the talents of other gifted pupils. You need to be on the look out for underachieving pupils who do not get the chance to communicate their talents, particularly in the way they would like to, who find the tasks too easy to let their talents shine, or who are bored because the learning tasks appear to lack purpose.

7   **Try not to have preconceptions.** A pupil may appear able if they speak confidently, have good vocabulary, act in a mature way and have good general knowledge. By contrast you might think a child who does not have these will not be gifted, but you could be overlooking something. You should also consider whether you have mechanisms in place for recognizing underachievers whose potential is high.

8   **Think creatively.** Provision and teaching approaches need to be flexible to meet the needs of such pupils. You could think about organizing paired/shared learning with two pupils who will stretch each other's talents. Alternatively, free groupings which allows them to stay with friends may motivate them more. You should consider enabling an able pupil to experience failure so that they appreciate challenge and success all the more. It is very important to give feedback on their learning, perhaps by marking their work with them. Talent needs to be recognized and success celebrated and accepted without embarrassment.

9   **Operate differentiation with the more able in mind**. There are four
    different types or levels of differentiation: by *outcome*, where the same
    task is set for all and different responses identify pupils' ability; *by rate of
    progress*, which allows pupils to work through a course at a slower or
    faster pace; *by enrichment*, when supplementary tasks are set to deepen or
    broaden understanding; and *by setting different tasks*, in the case of gifted
    pupils, those which have greater sophistication than the tasks others are
    doing.

10 **Give them applied tasks**. Able pupils need to have time and opportunity
    to pursue a variety of interests in depth. You can help by giving them a
    practical, real problem to solve. You should also encourage them to pursue
    their own interests. It is very important that you create time for them to
    'brainstorm' and interact with classmates so that they are a real part of
    the class, not isolated by their exceptionality.

27

Identifying pupils with Attention Deficit Disorder

You may find it helpful to identify a pupil with Attention Deficit Disorder by the following questions. If you can identify about seven of these as present in the pupil's behaviour over a period of six months, then you should think about contacting the school's educational psychologist. Make a note of occasions when they display these characteristics and talk to other staff about this. The educational psychologist will find it helpful if you can give more information about the pupil's behaviour in school, and whether the parent has concerns about this at home. If there is evidence that the pupil's work is affected by lack of attention, try to have examples ready to show them. This disorder usually begins in infancy and produces negative effects on their school, home and social life. In particular, it is characterized by severe difficulties in attention span and impulsive behaviour.

1   **Does the pupil fidget, squirm or seem restless?** You might think this applies more to the younger pupil, but it can be evident even in a late teenager. If so, try to sit them where they are least able to become distracted, near the front and you, in a firm seat that doesn't creak, with their back to the rest of the class.

2   **Does the pupil move from one incomplete task to another?** It may help if you set only one task at a time. Monitor the pupil's work frequently so that they know you will notice if they have moved to a different task. Give rewards for completed tasks, not incomplete ones.

3   **Does the pupil have difficulty sitting in one place?** Establish a group of role model pupils and friends that sit beside this pupil regularly so that they have a sense of what is their routine seating area. Avoid having other stimuli in this area, or elsewhere in other areas in the room, that might tempt the pupil away.

4   **Is the pupil easily distracted?** Try to avoid unnecessary interruptions or disruptions; you may need to talk to other staff and pupils about helping you with this. You may find it helpful to carry out an audit of your room for distractions: heaters, doors, windows, extractor fans, telephones, pupil and staff thoroughfares.

5   **Does the pupil talk excessively?** You will find it helps to have a routine that everyone follows about speaking out aloud; perhaps have a set of ground rules which are clearly displayed on the wall. Set a pattern for when they can talk, for example, allow them the chance to feed back what they have understood, particularly in relation to instructions.

6   **Does the pupil have difficulty in waiting for a turn for attention?** You may find it helpful to set up some kind of peer tutoring or support, which allows the pupil more immediate access to someone who will listen and explain the work. This collaborative learning can teach the pupil with attention deficit disorder the value of sharing.

7   **Does the pupil fail to listen to instructions or what others say?** You may need to simplify complex instructions or answers that others have given. Avoid giving multiple instructions. Repeat the essentials in a calm, positive clear manner. Provide written or visual reinforcement where possible.

8   **Does the pupil find it impossible to follow what needs to be done?** This can result in wasted effort and the frustration of working on completely the wrong thing. You may find that seating them near pupils who are reliable, and whom the pupil with Attention Deficit Disorder recognizes as good examples to follow, can help to keep the pupil on the right track. You may need to modify or differentiate the work so that they can achieve success before frustration.

9   **Does the pupil often lose equipment for a task or forget to bring it in?** Give the pupil a checklist for your lesson of everything they will need. If they require something extra, write it down for them and their parents. Try to encourage them to have a larger checklist or 'Don't Forget' list on their bedroom wall, or near the door by which they leave their house.

10 **Does the pupil find it hard to play quietly and sensibly?** They may be rejected by peers because of this and their classroom behaviour. They often behave so impulsively that others are frightened off by them and don't feel comfortable around them, never knowing what to expect next. You can help by establishing firm ground rules for behaviour with 'sanctions' that apply at the time, not later, so the pupil can see the direct consequences of their actions.

28

Attention Deficit Hyperactivity Disorder (ADHD)

Attention Deficit Hyperactivity Disorder may seem a relatively new term, and to some teachers it will seem to be a description of a pupil they might otherwise describe as both lazy and attention seeking. The ADHD pupil is on the same continuum as the Attention Deficit Disordered pupil, but has the added difficulty of hyperactive tendencies. It is thought that a probable cause lies in the neurological functions and, as such, can be treated with medication. Since inattentiveness, impulsiveness and hyperactivity can be found in other pupils, it is important to establish appropriate assessment through the Educational Psychology Service and specialist medical advice. The following tips relate to characteristics which are similar to those for an Attention Deficit Disordered pupil, but are more specific in areas of hyperactivity.

1   **Keep the pupil safe.** If the pupil seems restless or fidgety to the extent that they can become involved in dangerous actions, you will need to take appropriate action. This is often because they do not think through the consequences. Try to avoid placing the pupil near any stimuli which in themselves can prove dangerous, for example, some types of equipment, windows, sockets and cables, or other pupils who have behavioural problems.

2   **Recognize achievements.** If the pupil is distracted by extraneous stimuli over which you have no control, you need to minimize the effects of these stimuli, but acknowledge that the pupil will have to try especially hard to ignore them. Be sure to praise the pupil for ignoring them and encourage the pupil to monitor how well they did.

3   **Help the pupil to be patient in waiting for turns.** Let them know you have noticed them, so that frustration does not cause them to lose self-control. Try to establish eye contact that informs the pupil you know they are waiting and you will be with them soon. Be sure to follow this up with praise and self-evaluation of this success.

4 **Establish supervision and discipline into the pupil's routine.** If the pupil shouts out answers before being asked, you need to let them know the consequences of calling out. If you can impose a calm, measured approach in your teaching which is consistent, pupils can learn from your routine. Perhaps adopt a signal for the whole class that tells them when they can answer or whose turn it is to answer.

5 **Establish with the pupil the notion of what constitutes completed work if the pupil fails to finish work.** They may not recognize when they have properly completed the work, rather than just abandoned it. A record book of their completed tasks may motivate them to meet these requirements.

6 **Encourage them to ask for assistance so that they do not move on simply because they are stuck.** Pupils will often move from one activity to another whenever they experience difficulties. Unless you make a habit or routine of letting the pupil know when their work is complete, they will not understand the concept of completion.

7 **Help them to establish the habit of working quietly.** This needs to be reinforced with the help of parents; establishing a quiet study place at home where the pupil expects to work for set periods of time, perhaps ten or fifteen minute blocks, will help establish continuity of work space and time at school. You should try to have regular feedback about this, giving encouragement as well as reward.

8 **Modify the pupil's work so that they are able to work independently using their strengths.** The pupil who interrupts others, or intrudes on their activities and distracts others as a consequence, has little attention to give to the task in hand. It may be a good idea if you place the pupil near others who you know will not be so distracted, but who will be able to give guidance.

9 **Check back with the pupil regularly to see that they have been listening if the pupil seems not to listen to what is said.** Get them to repeat instructions and salient points at regular intervals to keep them focused. Let them know that you will be doing this, giving them a time budget to work towards, but avoid creating stress by giving them realistic time limits.

10 **Keep a small container at each pupil's work space with their essential equipment ready so every pupil can make a start on a task.** The pupil with Attention Deficit Hyperactivity Disorder often loses homework, pens, books, and so on, and may leave equipment behind, claim others have taken it from them, and so on. If you provide the basics in an ordered way, this teaches them a system they can adopt elsewhere. It also creates the sense that everything is in its correct place, and promotes an ordered existence to which they can respond.

29

Autistic Spectrum Disorders

This term applies to a range of language and communication disorders which overlap. Language development or non-verbal behaviour may be disproportionately impaired from one pupil to another. It is difficult to define the exact nature of one pupil's disabilities alongside that of another, and yet they fall within the same continuum. Thus, they are increasingly seen as a pattern of symptoms rather than specific conditions. It may be helpful, however, to distinguish between an autistic pupil with non-verbal or limited verbal communication and a pupil with Asperger's Syndrome. Characteristically an autistic person may have a high IQ or a highly developed skill strength such as music or art. You may find the following questions helpful in identifying or working with a pupil with autism. Remember, autism should not be seen as a label, but as a signpost directing you to meeting the pupil's needs and full psychological and medical advice should be sought.

1 **Does the pupil have difficulty relating to people?** The pupil may have a problem relating to you and other pupils. They might seem aloof, or passive, or even active, but odd. You and the pupils might find them eccentric in some way. They don't really have an understanding of socializing with other people, but this in itself does not distress them, unless someone makes an issue of it. Avoid situations where they have to be picked to join in, for example, a team.

2 **Does the pupil have difficulty with speech?** Difficulties can range here from no interest in communicating to repetitive language, irrelevant but factual contributions, a self-motivated need to communicate, incessant talk, strange use of language rules, and so on. This can be tough for a teacher to work with, and you may wish to seek specialist help to explore how best to manage this behaviour in the classroom.

3 **Does the pupil have difficulty interpreting speech and actions?** You will notice that an autistic pupil takes things very literally and you need to be careful that you don't upset them as a result. Avoid sarcasm, think about the literal meaning of what you say. If you ask them to 'hang on for a minute', they will wonder what they have to hang on to and will count to 60.

4   **Does the pupil have difficulty in responding to events or objects in the environment?** The pupil may find it hard to see things from your point of view or anyone else's. They have no flexibility of thought and behaviour. They have great difficulty adapting to changes. You may find they cannot generalize, but focus on the specific. Help them to feel safe in the classroom by staying calm and establishing routines.

5   **Does the pupil perform repetitive and stereotyped actions.** You may have observed the pupil going through an almost ritual-like performance in a given situation, perhaps on entering the classroom or getting equipment out. This routine never alters and if disrupted can upset them greatly, so avoid doing so.

6   **Does the pupil demonstrate a strong desire to keep things the same?** Little things can affect an autistic pupil such as a change in seat, an extraneous noise, the feel of particular clothing which is unfamiliar. You should try not to overload them with new experiences or changes in routine. This can cause them to have an outburst, so try to be aware of their stress levels.

7   **Does the pupil have a good memory, particularly for rote learning?** An autistic pupil remembers visual things particularly well, and finds it easier to remember the last lesson by picturing what another pupil did or said. They need 'cues' to help them remember, but once they have these, you can use them as a trigger repeatedly.

8   **Does the pupil have good cognitive potential?** Often the pupil will have the skills, but not the understanding to use them appropriately. You can help by giving them the context in which to exercise the skills. Try to make the context or situation as structured as possible, so they can relate to it more easily next time. They often have a poor sense of themselves and hate failure, so try to avoid putting red crosses on their work.

9   **Does the pupil have a weak sense of finish?** You need to give these kinds of pupil an understanding of when they have completed something, so don't leave it open-ended. If you ask a question to which you want more than a 'yes' or 'no' answer, then think about the wording. Help them by saying less, but make it unambiguous.

10   **Does the pupil have good coordination when handling objects?** The autistic pupil can dismantle and reassemble an intricate object with great ease and may have an obsessive need to repeat this again and again. There is a high level of built-in reward and success in doing this, so explore ways to build this kind of task into the work you provide for them.

30

Asperger's Syndrome

The pupil with Asperger's Syndrome may be much more difficult to recognize because they appear to have acquired speech and language structure in a normal way, but they still show signs of autism and they have difficulty in their social use of language. They are more likely to be in a mainstream school and expected to follow National Curriculum work. As suggested elsewhere in the book, the advice and assessment support of an educational psychologist and doctor are likely to be invaluable and necessary for a full diagnosis, but you might find the following tips help with focusing the pupil into achieving success within the curriculum.

1   **If the pupil is unable to get started on written work, isolate one small aspect of work and write the title/sub-heading in place.** Translate the activity into more diagrammatic form, for example, a table where they can fill in related details under headings.

2   **If the pupil has an obsession, or seems perpetually to be fiddling with equipment, acknowledge this.** It may even be helpful to express an interest in the object of obsession, but give them a set time when they can focus on it. Try to draw out a specific interest in their written work.

3   **Recognize when the pupil's mind or conversation is on a different activity.** Try to divert back to the subject in hand by cross-referencing. Don't force the issue, however, as this could lead to an outburst. Instead tell the pupil you will return to the other activity with them within a set time, so they can get ready for the change of focus.

4   **Avoid insisting on verbal response if the pupil refuses to speak.** Allow for non-verbal signal, explain that to the pupil, for example, 'If you understand then open your book …' or, 'I'll give you a few minutes to get underway, then I'll come and see how you are doing…'

5   **If a pupil seems unable to stay seated, offer limited opportunities for movement.** Try asking the pupil to do a small job for you that justifies their moving about, but say clearly that after this they need to get back to their seat and work on the set task.

6   **If the pupil refuses to do the work, even after these strategies have been tried, try another tack.** You could, for example, try giving them their own personal written instruction about what to do next. An autistic pupil will often find themselves unable to avoid carrying out such an instruction, even though they will still be maintaining they are not going to do it! If this works, give more of these prompts – be sure they are short and have a definite finish – the pupil may continue to come back for more against their own will!

7   **If the pupil seems unwilling to respond to any attempts to help, offer a get out.** Suggest they continue their work for the lesson with a member of staff designated as a 'sanctuary' at this time. Often an autistic pupil finds the noise and actions in a classroom too stressful to be able to concentrate; they need a minimum of stimuli to focus on work.

8   **If the pupil is aware of feeling in a strange mood and of the need to work elsewhere, listen to what is said.** You may find that the pupil is able to tell you they feel in a particular mood in which they are likely to have outbursts and confrontations. Respond to this, and organize it so they can work with a teacher with whom they feel comfortable and in an environment they feel at home in.

9   **Don't ignore it if you are aware that the pupil is causing you, or the rest of the class, to say or do things you feel may get out of hand.** It can be that there are days, or times in the day, when you know that you or another teacher has been stretched and do not have the patience to keep on top of the situation. Respond to this, and arrange that the pupil can work away from this situation. Teachers are allowed to feel under stress and avoid confrontations with a pupil who has very demanding needs.

10   **Try to think and plan the words really carefully before you say something.** Ask yourself if the pupil might take it literally. Remember, such pupils cannot understand irony or some types of humour. If you think you are in danger of confusing them, say less.

31

Dyslexia

Dyslexia, literally meaning 'difficulty with words', is a term that describes the symptoms rather than the causes of a range of specific learning difficulties. Dyslexia has no single cause and may result from underlying physiological or developmental conditions. Regrettably, it is frequently and loosely used by parents and teacher alike as a catch-all term for those who have difficulties with spelling or reading. The diagnosis of dyslexia requires an assessment by an educational psychologist; however, the following questions may help you to recognize some of the indicators a dyslexic pupil might display. A significant combination of these could merit you referring the situation to the appropriate person at your school for example, the SENCO, who should then discuss with you whether to contact the Educational Psychology Service.

1   **Does the pupil's written work regularly contain a high level of spelling mistakes?** This is perhaps the most obvious indicator you will find. However, the pupil may still spell out aloud correctly. Are the correct letters used, but in the wrong order? Does the spelling make sense using a phonic approach, for example, 'w-o-z' for 'was'?

2   **Does the pupil have difficulty sequencing?** You may recognize this already as part of the spelling problem, for example, the use of the correct letters in the wrong order. The sequencing difficulty can also be more widespread: sequencing words in a sentence incorrectly; carrying out instructions in the wrong order; getting the shape of letters back to front, for example, writing or reading 'b' for 'd', 'p' for 'q' or 'god' for 'dog'; difficulty remembering the sequence of days of the week and months of the year; patterns of numbers in ascending or descending order, '316' for '613'.

3   **Does the pupil have problems remembering what has been said to them?** We all have a short-term memory system. Some people are naturally better at remembering and understanding what they hear than what they see. However, a dyslexic pupil may have a greater difficulty recalling what you have just said. In contrast they might be good at recalling what they have just seen.

4   **Does the pupil have problems remembering what they have seen?**
     Conversely, it may be a real struggle for the pupil to draw or copy
     something that you have presented visually, causing problems copying
     from the board. With handwriting, unless the letter or word shape is drawn
     lightly underneath, they cannot form it properly, yet they may have no
     problems recalling what you have just said.

5   **Does the pupil appear clumsy in either fine or gross motor skills?** Have
     you noticed that the pupil finds it difficult to draw delicate patterns, keep
     to a line or within borders when writing? The same problem may be
     present with larger movements, such as walking or balancing; they may
     knock into things and fail to judge distances well.

6   **Does the pupil find rhyme and rhythm difficult to maintain?** Have you
     noticed that the pupil finds it very hard to recognize similar sounds, or
     understand the shape of their mouth when they make certain sounds.
     Similarly, they may find it difficult to recognize similar feelings of
     movement and pace in a rhythm. This can also affect their ability to
     remember the correct feel of a letter, whole word shape, even of regularly
     used words such as their own name.

7   **Does a preference for left dominance occur in one or more of the sensory
     areas?** Does the pupil have difficulty distinguishing left from right? The
     pupil may use the left hand for writing, but have a right dominance
     elsewhere. Do they throw with their left or right hand, kick or hop with
     their left or right leg, look through a microscope with the left or right eye,
     listen to a single sound source with left or right ear? If they have a confused
     dominance, it could hinder their learning. You may also have noticed a
     form of 'mirror' writing.

8   **Is the pupil's overall level of performance lower than that you would
     expect?** You may find this easier to detect in the more able pupil, but the
     pupil does not have to be able for dyslexia to be a consideration; a slower
     learner may also show a discrepancy between their apparent ability and
     overall progress or performance. You probably know less able pupils for
     whom you feel disappointment when they cannot match on paper what
     they can in speech.

9   **Does the pupil lack concentration and demonstrate restlessness or
     hyperactivity?** You will recognize the pupil who finds it hard to settle to
     an activity, and is ready for a change in activity much earlier than others
     in the class. This pupil may also find it hard to plan an essay or piece of
     writing, even harder to apply a pattern of organization to their notes or
     activities.

10   **Is there a family history of similar difficulties?** You often find that once these difficulties are discussed, the pupil or parent may inform you that someone else in the family suffers from similar difficulties.

32

Supporting pupils with language impairment

As teachers, we tend to take the use of language for granted, because it is such a central part of our lives. However, for a sizeable minority of children, the acquisition of verbal language is not straightforward, and the subsequent language impairment represents a specific learning difficulty. The following suggestions are designed to help you in your support of these pupils.

1   **Break down verbal instructions.** Keep them short. Do not assume comprehension. Give instructions in small steps. Ask pupils to repeat instructions back to you. This will give you a chance to recast the sentence into a better model. The pupil may say, 'I have to write on that volcano thing'. You can now say, 'Good. You have to label all the parts of the volcano diagram using the correct words'.

2   **Cue your pupil in to each new stage of the lesson.** You could hold up a book to point to a heading or a picture. You can also point with your finger to the appropriate paragraph in the pupil's book. If you are giving verbal information, you could touch the pupil lightly on the hand or shoulder and say, 'You need to listen very carefully now'.

3   **Encourage good personal organization skills.** Make sure that pupils understand that they have sole responsibility for being in the right place at the right time. You could check if they have their timetables and all their equipment ready for the day's lessons. Perhaps you can provide your pupils with achievable daily or weekly targets.

4   **Enable pupils to help themselves.** Perhaps they will need a teacher to repeat or clarify information. Teach your pupil how to explain what they have not understood. For example the pupil can have a stock of phrases such as 'What does... mean?' or, 'What do I have to do first?' or, 'I don't know what that word means' or, 'I don't understand'.

5   **Improve attention and listening skills.** Try to ensure that your pupil, who has difficulty communicating, sits in a good listening position. You could also send pupils to deliver messages. In group listening work, you could appoint your pupil to provide verbal feedback on the group's opinions. One way to ensure careful listening is to tell stories, or give information with deliberate mistakes which must be corrected.

6   **Give good visual and contextual clues.** Pupils may often know the answer to a question, but are unable to find the right words to reply. You could present questions in alternative ways. For instance, you could say, 'What did Fleming discover? Was it penicillin or x-rays?' You can also prompt answers by sounding the first letter or syllable of the required word.

7   **Improve written response.** For instance, you could introduce new vocabulary with a definition and a visual clue. Give exercises which provide useful practice in processing information, such as use of contents and index pages, timetables, dictionaries, encyclopaedias and reference books. Cloze and sequencing exercises provide good practice in word skills, and writing frames can provide a supporting structure for written work.

8   **Aim for a continuous improvement in vocabulary.** Recap constantly on new vocabulary and do not assume it will be remembered immediately. You could encourage pupils to keep vocabulary notebooks. Aim for the pupil to learn perhaps ten key words in each topic area. Develop understanding and use of adjectives.

9   **Avoid the use of open-ended questions.** Be aware that complicated linguistic structures may cause confusion. Try to give the pupil a clear choice of answer. Don't teach grammar and vocabulary out of context. Keep sentences short and simple. Aim for one piece of information per sentence.

10 **Speech disorders should not be confused with language impairment.** Pupils who have speech impediments, or who may be elective mutes, are suffering from physical or emotional problems and will already be under the supervision of specialists. Check with your SENCO if you are in any doubt.

Language impairment – checklist of concern

The following checklist (based on guidelines by Beveridge, M and Conti-Ramsden, G *Children and Language Disabilities*(1987) OUP, Buckingham) may be indicators of a language and communication difficulty, if a number of them occur regularly in a variety of contexts and situations.

Does the pupil *regularly:*

- Misunderstand simple instructions, either spoken or written?
- Make errors when reading aloud?
- Have difficulty in keeping track of conversations?
- Find it difficult to complete unfinished sentences appropriately?
- Find it difficult to make the correct 'how', 'why', 'what if' and 'what next' inferences?
- Produce odd grammatical structures when either speaking and/or writing?
- Not seem to understand fully logical connectives like 'because', 'therefore', 'so if – then', 'however' and 'although'?
- Not seem to get the gist of what has been said; not know what many things read or heard are about?
- Have poor memory for linguistically presented information?
- Fail to make connections between what has been read or heard?
- Talk in a roundabout and vague way, often not completing sentences and repeating him or herself?
- Become difficult to understand in terms of the sounds used as language demands increase?
- Avoid tasks and situations involving language?
- Seem slow to respond to instructions to a group and depend on social cues?
- Go off the point, only talk about one or two subjects which interest him or her?
- Have a poor awareness of audience, speak inappropriately or with over familiarity to strangers?

33

Dyspraxia

In the past pupils with Dyspraxia were probably described as clumsy. Now there is a recognition that there is more to it than just that, and there are tell-tale signs and ways teachers and parents can help. Dyspraxia is classed as a Specific Learning Difficulty, in that it is an impairment of movement and coordination through the mechanisms that control these areas of activity. As such, it can also affect language perception and thought, as well as speech. These tips are designed to help you to recognize and support pupils with dyspraxia. At the same time, you are urged to ensure that an educational psychologist and doctor have been consulted.

1   **If the pupil has poor gross and fine motor coordination, consult your occupational therapist for advice.** You will have come across the pupil who seems unable to coordinate successfully the actions of the whole body or parts of the body. This pupil probably has difficulty in PE. Occupational therapists can devise programmes to help this pupil to develop their fine and gross motor coordination. You can help by allowing some leeway with presentation of work, perhaps letting them write on alternate lines.

2   **If the pupil has difficulties with balance and is accident prone, avoid overloading the pupil with physical tasks which require complex dexterity.** Instead give simple carrying or collecting jobs. Again the occupational therapist will have programmes designed to help awareness of touch, sense of body position and movement. As long as you are aware of these, you might help by building in activities which complement them, but check with the occupational therapist.

3   **Help pupils who have poor spatial and conceptual understanding of Maths.** Dyspraxic pupils tend to have poor spatial discrimination, so they find it hard to read mathematical sums and interpret the symbols, concepts and processes involved. Similarly, they will have difficulty writing figures in the correct place to create a sum that has correct value. You could help

by providing large squared paper to encourage correct number value and neater layout. Always check how much the pupil has understood before moving on.

4   **Provide opportunities for pupils to improve poorly developed social skills.** They may need a programme to manage daily activities. This could involve learning routes around school, how to change into and out of PE kit more quickly, how to handle school dinner queues, dinner trays, and so on. You might make this easier for the pupil if you can encourage a friend to act as a 'buddy', someone who will watch out for them and help out if they see difficulties or failure looming.

5   **Use a multi-sensory approach where the pupil has poor reading, writing and spelling skills, and has books which are messy.** You can help the pupil store what they have been taught more effectively by doing this through the different sensory areas simultaneously. This in turn makes it easier to recall the information, because there are several sources of information; sight, sound, touch, and so on. You can have a lot of fun teaching this way, and it helps to motivate the pupil.

6   **Provide face-saving support for pupils who have difficulties in PE.** If the pupil has balance and coordination problems, you may find it helps if you allow them to work with a partner and select appropriate games, activities and apparatus. To avoid embarrassment, you could suggest that everyone works with partners at first, then allow this pupil to continue. You will need to be careful about choice of partner and how to encourage team work. The occupational therapist may also be able to give exercises that can help improve these areas.

7   **Be aware that some pupils may have difficulties with dressing and undressing.** You will need to work on this with parents, relevant teachers and an occupational therapist. This pupil will have difficulty with fastenings, and coordinating and balancing the body as items of clothing need to be handled. You can help them by reminding them of the best order of actions. Sometimes it helps to have the clothes laid out ready in this order, but at school they will need to know this for themselves to save embarrassment.

8   **Differentiate materials where pupils have poor concentration and attention spans.** It will help if the pupil has shorter tasks to complete, including homework. Allow the use of aids such as a word-processor, a calculator or a tape-recorder. If you mark this pupil as much on their verbal responses as on their written ones, it will give more scope for progress.

9   **Be aware that dyspraxia may lead to behavioural problems.** A dyspraxic pupil often has difficulty filtering out background noises and distractions, so they may appear to ignore others and continue with another activity. Their behaviour may seem disruptive and impulsive. It may help if you let them know that you are aware of their difficulties, and try to prepare them in advance for changes of activities, and so on. Their understanding of concepts of time can also lead to misunderstandings.

10 **Take account of the often poor perceptual skills of dyspraxic pupils, who may have difficulties in understanding differences between shapes.** The dyspraxic pupil has great difficulty copying writing, keeping letters on the line, positioning writing on the page, spacing letters and words, judging the end of a line and drawing a letter or shape in one continuous movement. You can help them by allowing ample time, reading and checking work with them, and marking their work on content not presentation. At the same time, it might help if you can be positive about even little areas of progress and give plenty of praise and encouragement.

34

Tips for improving reading

If you have pupils whose reading age is significantly lower than their chronological age (three years or more), they are likely to need an intensive, structured course of corrective reading. Ideally, this course should contain the following elements, if you are to motivate the pupil and actually bring about improvement in reading skills, self-esteem and confidence.

1   **Provide support on a regular daily basis.** Regular reinforcement is vital if the pupil is to recall new information. Time should be spent reviewing the previous day's work, but this will be easier to achieve if the sessions are daily. Twenty minutes reading a day amounts to five days a year of additional reading support.

2   **Timetable reading time as early as possible in the day, when both you and the pupil are fresh.** The pupil needs to see that priority is being given to their needs. Encourage their prompt attendance with rewards such as certificates or, if the school's policy allows, treats at the end of the week for good, punctual attendance that week.

3   **Allow a significant time for the reading sessions.** Less than twenty minutes will not allow for more than simple reading for pleasure. This pupil will need you to teach them more specific rules and strategies for improvement. This is best approached if there is a structure. The pupil needs to know that they will not be expected to read words, unless they have been taught and are prepared to understand and recognize particular letter patterns and their sounds.

4   **Keep the size of the reading group small.** There should be enough time so that every pupil within it has individual reading time and tuition. You need to ensure that no one in the group waits more than five or six minutes before they have a turn to practise reading. Listening to others reading is valuable, but you must remain aware of the optimum time that a pupil's attention for listening can be maintained. For a group of six or seven pupils, a daily time of forty minutes allows for individual reading practice and a change in task to maintain motivation.

5 **Avoid timetabling reading time at the expense of other lessons.** It may be inevitable, but you can minimize problems if there is cooperation and support at all levels in the structure of school management. An arrangement that shares the time between two points of the school day, perhaps registration and Period One each day, spreads the disruption across the curriculum so that no one area suffers regularly.

6 **Give careful consideration to where the reading group meets.** You may find that these pupils are very sensitive to their needs being made obvious to their peers. Try to use a room that is not on a route used by pupils moving between lessons; let it be known that you don't want interruptions and try not to leave the door open or ajar. Build up the pupils' self-esteem by giving the sessions a high profile in their day, and indicate to them that they are special in your day.

7 **Consider structured phonics teaching as part of the course.** In this way, pupils can see they are building up a knowledge of the rules and uses of letter sounds. You can help them gain confidence to read by sound building; when faced with an unfamiliar word, they will know they can turn to the familiar knowledge of certain sound patterns.

8 **Create a bank of common sight words to add a further dimension to their confidence.** You can spend a little time each day on the commonly used words that occurred in the reading passage, which do not seem to follow standard phonic patterns.

9 **Have fun with mnemonics.** Round off the reading session with 'fun' ways of remembering some tricky words; you could use the board to draw pictures that visualize a word and help the pupil pronounce it correctly. Perhaps you could build up a pack of cards with these for each pupil. For instance, you could draw a baby howling to remind them that 'ow' in clown, town, drown, brown, etc have the same sound. Put each word inside a tear drop on the drawing. Think up different images to differentiate the 'ow' in snow, glow, slow and so on.

10 **Celebrate important occasions.** These might include a birthday, the end of term, test marks improvement, or whatever. If you have tested the pupil for reading age at the start of the course, give regular feedback by re-testing and discussing results. Allow the pupil to take a special book home, let the birthday boy or girl select a book or particular passage to read, reward them with a book mark, certificate, and so on. If you follow a structured course, award a certificate at key stages in the course.

35

Tips for improving spelling

Traditionally, it may seem that teachers have taught spelling by grouping words into families and giving lists of words to learn for a test. In truth, it has never been that simple or straightforward. Some pupils have an inability to learn spellings off by heart or by rote, while others may learn them sufficiently to remember the patterns in a test the next day, only to have no recollection of them two days later. These tips are designed to help you to find ways of helping each pupil to find successful long-term strategies for spelling.

1   **Find out the sensory channel that works best for the pupil.** You will need to know whether the pupil remembers what they *see* or what they *hear* more effectively. Try to discover which letter patterns have been established in the pupil's memory. You can use these as a framework on which to hang other spelling families; you could even design a pack of cards for each family.

2   **Use board games and card games.** These are particularly successful for those who have weak visual skills. You can make your own games, but there are a number of really interesting commercial ones that are equally effective. You could consider using these as a final ten-minute activity in a lesson already devoted to spelling work or as a reminder of the last lesson's content.

3   **Use a structured programme of spelling patterns.** This will act in the same way as a structured reading programme, allowing the pupil to progress at the rate at which they feel comfortable. The pupils know they will not be faced with exercises in your lesson that they are likely to fail at. They will gain confidence from knowing that anything you expect them to spell correctly contains a pattern you have already taught them.

4   **Create a series of subject-specific spelling cards.** These can give the pupil a tangible sense of coping with their individual subject demands. You can help pupils do this by going through their subject exercise, or text books, and writing 10 words per card that have 'tricky' spellings, or which are commonly misspelt by the pupil. These can be kept on hand when doing homework, or even in lesson time assignments.

5   **Make up mnemonics.** Ones that stick in the mind because they are funny, they rhyme or are even slightly rude, can be another really useful part of your approach. You can build up your own bank of these with the pupil, but some well known ones already exist. 'Big Elephants Are Ugly' has helped many people remember the order of the first four letters in the word 'beautiful'.

6   **Avoid overloading the memory with lists of words to learn by rote.** You can encourage pupils to spell using reason and the knowledge of spelling rules. This can be made easier by always encouraging them to break the word down into syllable sounds or short manageable units.

7   **Encourage a sensory approach.** In this way, the pupil learns to read, say, sound and write the word. You need to pay particular attention to the kinaesthetic sense. Most people could write their own names correctly, even with their eyes closed, because it feels right. A pupil needs to grow used to the right feel of a word.

8   **Encourage the use of a spell checker whenever the pupil is allowed to employ this facility in his school work or coursework.** You might also give consideration to other information technology accessories, such as software that predicts the word the pupil wants to use from the first few letters typed in.

9   **Make appropriate use of dictionaries.** Telling a child with spelling difficulties to look the word up in a dictionary can be very demoralizing, they may even find it too difficult to locate the first few letters. You could suggest that the child tries using a dictionary specially designed to match their processes in decoding a word. A dictionary like this will have been aurally coded.

10   **Check spelling backwards.** You can try to encourage the pupil to proof read their work but this can be more effective if you tell them to work backwards through the passage! This is not as mad as it sounds. When you read forwards though a passage you see what you expect to read in terms of meaning, and therefore do not note a spelling error. If you read backwards, each word and its spelling stands on its own and you become more aware of an incorrect appearance.

36

Paired reading

Paired reading is, as the name suggests, a way of encouraging and improving reading by getting a stronger reader to pair up with the weak reader and spend time together sharing the reading. The 'paired reader' could be a parent, a friend or, if the school has the facility, another pupil, possibly from a different year group. The type of pupil you might place with a paired reader needs encouragement and confidence to read more fluently. They may be a year or two behind their chronological age in reading, but not so far behind that they need a structured course. The following tips are suggestions for how this scheme can operate successfully, particularly in a secondary school, and propose some of the other benefits which such a scheme can bring.

1   **Go for 'little and often'.** As little as five minutes a day can be sufficient to encourage fluency. You will probably find that 15 minutes is the maximum time the pupil will want to read for. You would be advised not to make the pupil do paired reading when they would rather be doing something else, or they will grow up to associate reading with not enjoying themselves.

2   **Find a place that is quiet and has few distractions, such as television.** This can be hard to achieve in a school, particularly if you try to have a group of paired readers. If you can, you need to find a room which is away from other classrooms, but one which the pupils can get to on time. Alternatively you could encourage paired reading in class registration time, where all the pupils in a class can choose from a tub of books.

3   **Let the pupil choose the book and you will find they enjoy it all the more.** Try to have a selection of books that are age appropriate for the paired readers to choose from. If they choose one that is too hard, they will put this right themselves. However, it may help if you have a system of coding for the books, so that you know the reading age of the book and, ideally, be on hand to advise.

4 **Keep the books looking good.** Attractive looking books which have been kept in good condition appeal far more to a reluctant reader. If you set up a reading tub in each classroom, try to make sure that the books all have plastic covers. Organize a system so that the books are handed out and collected in, and that way the tub is kept tidy. You can encourage more enjoyment by using bookmarks and stickers on a colourful chart/ catalogue.

5 **Read at the pace at which the pupil reads.** It is very important not to read too fast. The pupil will read at the speed with which they can cope. Be patient and listen, try not to take over. You will notice when they start to read more fluently, and they will also notice and feel good, but it will mean even more to them if you tell them how much they have improved.

6 **Organize how the paired reading will work.** You might decide that the readers should actually read together at the same time. It will help if one of the readers points to the words as they are read. If the child gets a word wrong, or struggles for a while to work it out, then help them out. It can be embarrassing and discouraging to them if the pupil struggles for more than five seconds, simply say the word and get them to repeat it.

7 **Decide on a cue for reading alone.** When the pupil feels ready to read on their own, it can help them to have a signal that they want to do this. If you actually stop to say something, you can lose the sense of the words. Maybe a tap on the desk, or a 'thumbs up', could be the cue. Once started, you may find they don't want to stop reading.

8 **Remember that paired reading is designed for building up fluency and confidence not for teaching a structured course of phonics.** If you start to break words up into sound patterns, you run the risk of losing the spontaneity of reading, and the child may feel they have not got very far in the five or ten minutes set aside. You should think about teaching the phonics in another lesson if you feel the child really needs help with this.

9 **Concentrate on the matter in hand.** If you want to build in an activity other than reading, try talking about the book, but leave this until a suitable point in the text. Let the pupil choose what parts to talk about, even if it is the illustrations. You could also discuss what you both think will happen next, and then see who is right.

10 **Keep a paired reading diary.** It could become an end-of-week activity to write a diary entry between you. The diary could simply be a record of the book you are reading and the page number. However, you would probably find it more rewarding to write some comments about improvement, the story line, what you expect to happen next, and so on.

37

Being an effective learning support teacher in a mainstream classroom

As a peripatetic support teacher from a learning support service, you are likely to be required to work in a variety of classrooms in mainstream schools, supporting teachers you do not know in subjects with which you are not familiar. Even if you are an established support teacher who is on the school staff, the same conditions may apply. The following suggestions are designed to help you in this role.

1   **Aim for a successful first meeting with your mainstream colleague.** If you are a peripatetic learning support teacher, you will need to introduce yourself in advance of your arrival in the classroom. Make sure the teacher has read (or at least had access to) the Individual Education Plan (IEP) for your pupil and understands the reason for support. Check if the teacher has any worries about your presence in the classroom and offer reassurance.

2   **Arrange to liaise as soon as possible to discuss your aims and proposed strategies for supporting your pupil.** Check if your proposed mode of support is acceptable. Find out if you can work effectively with other pupils in the class and say what you can offer. Ask for schemes of future work in advance. If you are working in an unfamiliar subject area, ask for clarification of main aims and concepts.

3   **Arrange a meeting with your new pupils before you arrive in the classroom.** Ask for help in facilitating a private meeting. Give the pupils an opportunity to express any opinions or expectations about support. Adolescent pupils are often embarrassed about being identified in front of their peers as needing help. Take this into account by making a point of working with other pupils before you offer support to your target pupil.

4   **Check if the learning environment in the classroom will be beneficial to your pupil.** There may be noise and disruption, or the teacher may monopolize the entire lesson. Your role may become passive and ineffectual. Perhaps you could try removing your pupil along with a small group of pupils to a quieter environment. You could also suggest that it would be more helpful if you supported lessons where the emphasis was on literacy or practical skills.

5   **Try to avoid undermining the authority of your mainstream colleague.** Remember you are essentially the second string in this classroom. Do not intervene in disciplining pupils until you have tacit permission to do so. Pupils may try to manipulate you into countermanding some instruction of their teacher. Make it clear that their teacher is in charge of the class. Only intervene in obviously dangerous situations.

6   **Be aware of the necessity to behave with tact and diplomacy.** Try not to alienate a colleague who has made an error, by drawing attention to it in a tactless way. For example, a teacher may misspell a word which all the pupils are now copying into their books. You could circulate quietly around individuals correcting it and saying, 'I expect Miss didn't notice that' or, 'I always make mistakes when I'm writing on the board'. If the teacher appears flustered, make light of the error and sympathize. We all make mistakes, and perhaps your unaccustomed presence has added to the stress. Perhaps you might judge it better not to comment at all. After all, you are not there to assess the teacher, but to support your pupil and you are in need of this teacher's cooperation.

7   **Be aware of the possibility that you can marginalize your pupil and yourself.** One feature of support, which is often criticized, is when the support teacher sits exclusively with one pupil. Occasionally, it may be essential that you work that way, but it can also be helpful to your pupil if you circulate and support other pupils of all abilities.

8   **Offer your experience and time to produce differentiated materials for use with your pupil and others in the class.** However, before you produce large quantities of materials, check if the subject area is already well covered. If the class teacher has no experience in differentiating text, you could make suggestions for simple sequencing and Cloze procedures, and simplification of text and vocabulary.

9   **Be generous in sharing your resources.** You may have access to a resource bank which includes books, display materials, games and maybe even a laptop computer. However, do make sure you devise a foolproof system for the safe keeping and safe return of the materials.

10   **Support your mainstream colleague in practical ways.** Your own classroom teaching may be far in the past, but you will not have forgotten the daily routine. Make sure you arrive at lessons on time. Do not slip away if your pupil is absent. Avoid arranging meetings for difficult lessons which you would rather miss. Don't award yourself privileges which are not available to your colleague. Earn the respect of this teacher on whose support your effectiveness depends.

38

Identifying pupils who may be experiencing physical, emotional or sexual abuse

It is often really difficult for teachers to find ways of supporting pupils who they know, or suspect, to be experiencing some kind of abuse. Certainly, we are more aware nowadays of the prevalence of child abuse than was the case some years ago, but this doesn't make it any easier to handle. A first stage of helping pupils to find the support they need is identifying where the problems may lie, so that we can bring in specialist help where it is needed and provide support in the classroom to the best of our abilities.

1   **Be watchful of absenteeism.** As with many emotional and behavioural difficulties, absenteeism is a prime indicator that all is not well with your pupil. A long established pattern may already have been investigated, but you should check new and unexplained absences.

2   **Look for danger signals.** Pupils who rarely smile, seem withdrawn and detached, and who have few or no friends may be showing early or ongoing signs of abuse. Report your anxieties to pastoral and special needs staff. Try to discuss the problem with the pupil. You may get clues from the answers or lack of them.

3   **Watch behaviour in lessons.** Lethargy and even the tendency to sleep in lessons may indicate an incipient medical condition, an excessively over-active social life or possibly abuse of some kind. This may be accompanied by an unwillingness to take off outer clothing or to join in physical or group activities.

4   **Look for causes of anger.** Anger, aggression and disruptive behaviour in the classroom stem from many causes, but often the expression of anger towards teachers and peers is rooted in personal trauma. Anger towards an abuser, which cannot be articulated, is sometimes directed instead to others. Be as calm and reassuring as possible, and offer listening or counselling support.

5   **Remember that abused pupils may become excessively demanding or attention seeking.** This may result in disruptive classroom behaviour, but sometimes pupils, on finding a sympathetic teacher, may make unreasonable demands on their time and attention. Offer what you can in terms of cheerful support, but be clear and firm about where your boundaries lie.

6   **Look out for hypochondria.** This can be a way of gaining attention and sympathy. Some pupils may complain of a wide range of symptoms, and will be a familiar face to the school nurse or the long-suffering office staff. Try to remain patient in the face of this irritating behaviour. Perhaps you could say something on the lines of, 'Is there anything else that is troubling you?'

7   **Lack of basic cooperation in the classroom may indicate a troubled pupil.** Pupils may persistently refuse to cooperate in simple classroom management, and will only do things their way or in their own time, or not at all. They are classroom refusers rather than school refusers.

8   **Watch out for physical signs.** You may notice physical signs that your pupil is under stress. Pupils may have frequent and unexplained bruises, cuts or burns. Be vigilant about making non-threatening enquiries as to the cause of these injuries. Ask if your pupil needs help. A plausible explanation may be offered, but you may still be worried. Record and report your findings to pastoral staff.

9   **Look for any indicators of sexual abuse.** One indicator of sexual abuse is sexually explicit language and conversation in the playground, which may be making other pupils upset or angry, or at the very least they may find it noteworthy and rather surprising. Written work may reveal worrying information, which should be shared with appropriate colleagues and discussed with the pupil and the parents.

10 **Observe pupils reactions to teachers.** Behavioural indicators of sexual abuse may include uneasiness or hostility towards teachers of the opposite sex. Pupils may indulge in sexual bullying or sexual harassment of their peers. Prompt action should follow to prevent further harm to all your pupils.

11   **Ensure that your own behaviour is always appropriate.** Pupils who have been abused may mistake your disapproval for anger or your friendliness for attraction. Take sensible precautions to avoid making them feel any worse and to protect yourself from damaging accusations.

12   **Take seriously your own worries or anxieties.** If you feel there is something wrong, but you cannot quite formulate your anxiety, share your concern with a colleague you can trust. Abused pupils often find it difficult to disclose their traumas, but may give off signals that they hope someone will interpret. Obviously, use your common sense so as not to make rash false accusations, but trust your feelings.

Chapter 4 Tips for non-specialists on helping children with special needs

The following sets of tips are designed for teachers without specialist training, but working with pupils who have special needs, and want to be aware of the issues and to be able to provide informed support for their pupils, while knowing when to refer them on for additional specialist help. The tips may also be useful to parents of children with special needs, who want to do everything they can to help them to develop and thrive at school.

39 Identifying a special need: what should you be doing?
40 Identifying a special need: should you have known?
41 Working effectively in the classroom with a peripatetic learning support teacher
42 Identifying special needs: an alphabetical compendium

- Absences
- Absenteeism or truancy
- Antagonism
- Anti-social behaviour
- Attention seeking
- Attention span
- Bullying
- Calling out
- Cautious pupils
- Childishness
- Clumsiness
- Copying problems
- Defensiveness
- Defiance
- Examination phobia
- Excessively critical pupils

- Handwriting problems
- Hyperactivity
- Hypochondria
- Immaturity
- Insecurity
- Jokers
- Left-handedness
- ME
- Memory problems
- Moodiness
- Muscular dystrophy
- Nervousness
- Obsessive behaviour
- Outbursts
- Post-traumatic shock disorder
- Questioning everything

- Quiet pupils
- Rudeness
- Reading difficulties
- Self-mutilation and self-harm
- Sensory impairment
- Sequencing difficulties
- Sexually inappropriate behaviour
- Short concentration span
- Slow responses
- Speech difficulties
- Spelling difficulties
- Stutters
- Telling lies repeatedly
- Tired pupils
- Withdrawn pupils

39

Identifying a special need: what should you be doing?

Almost everyone has a special need at some time in their life, whether it is related to emotional, physical or learning situations, but it doesn't necessarily mean that special help should be sought. Many of these needs can be transitory, while others may have more lasting effects. It is sometimes hard to tell if there is a difficulty of which you, as a teacher, parent or carer, should be taking more notice. These questions are designed to help you to establish whether or not there is a special need.

1 **Can you describe the problem?** Try to write down as many things as you can that describe the way the problem manifests itself, and in what situations and at what times it comes to light. If you can pinpoint details like these, you can build strategies around this information that will help you and the pupil in the short term, and perhaps even in the long term.

2 **How long you have been aware of it?** If you know that it has been in the back of your mind for a while, write down some facts and discuss it with your pupil's other teacher(s) and those who may have taught them before. Decide between you whether it is sensible to talk about it to the pupil at this stage. Keep a record of the situation, so that you feel you are doing something positive.

3 **Has it just become more obvious?** Can you specify a particular time when it began, or when it became significantly worse? Has someone mentioned it to you, and if so what triggered their awareness? Try to identify other events that happened about the time when you became aware; do you think they could be connected? Remember that by identifying issues, you are already helping to find solutions.

4   **Is the pupil aware of it?** Has the pupil commented about the situation and, if so, have they seen it as a problem or just as a feature of their everyday life? If they see it as a problem, reassure them that you have listened and will think about what should be done. If they talk about it as just part of their life, then don't draw any more attention to it for now, but keep an eye on how often they refer to it and how they say it affects them when they are working, and so on.

5   **Do other pupils have similar problems?** If other pupils do have similar problems, which have recently come to light, it may be something specific that should be taken up with the school. If pupils have come to you, as a teacher, with problems that seem related, it may be linked to subject specific areas that you will need to talk to other teachers about.

6   **Have you tried talking to the pupil about it?** It can be reassuring to a pupil to learn that they are not the only one having problems. Discuss this with the pupil, and see if they can tell you why some pupils cope better. Even if it is only a small detail they tell you, it may give both of you a positive idea to try out.

7   **Does the difficulty actually limit the progress of the pupil?** Can you measure this? Has there been a significant change in the pupil's marks or standard of work and behaviour, such that you know progress is affected?

8   **Is there a difference between the pupil's standard of work orally and that which is written down?** Try to find out why the pupil can put something into words, but not write it down on paper. If you can see a difference in the content of the written work now and previously, try to list the good points that helped the pupil achieve success and progress in the past, so that you can suggest these as positive ways forward now.

9   **Will it cure itself?** This probably depends on what brought it about in the first place, but there could be a danger in thinking it is just a phase the pupil is going through because then you set no time limit on when it should end. A problem once identified should be monitored, in case it flares up again or gets worse.

10   **How long will it take to see some improvement?** Try to have time limits in mind as a trigger for your next course of action. However, ensure that they are reasonable. For example, one week is too short for any change to be noticeable, one month is probably more realistic, whilst half a term gives more time for a full evaluation of the problem in your mind and any monitoring that may need to be undertaken. If it has gone on for half a term, then it is significant enough to be making an appreciable difference to the pupil's education.

40

Identifying a special need: should you have known?

It can be difficult for a non-specialist teacher, let alone a parent or pupil, to identify specific indicators or symptoms and then to recognize them in special needs terminology. It can be even more difficult to decide what is the best course of action. It is very important that you do not feel guilty at any stage, either for not recognizing a special need, or for not doing something earlier. Parents and teachers who are not specialists working with pupils with special needs may find the following tips helpful in coming to a decision about whether to act or not, as well as providing some suggested strategies whatever decision is made.

1   **Don't just think, 'Others have this problem, so it can't be all that serious'.** It doesn't have to be unique for a problem to be significant. Recognizing that others appear to have the same problem may be a very positive step forward in identifying the cause, the contributory factors, the strategies that help overcome it and the approaches/remedies that really work.

2   **Take care not to assume that because some pupils cope with the problem that this pupil will cope in the same way.** Each need is individual to the person it affects, and they need to know that they have their own way of coping. So, while it can be reassuring to know that others have found ways of coping with the problem, you must convince the pupil that they should learn from this and develop their own strategies.

3   **Be cautious about assuming that identifying the problem is the solution.** Take care not to let yourself become convinced that every aspect of the pupil's performance is accounted for by having found a name for the problem, or that knowing this provides an answer. This won't be the case. Do not jump to the conclusion that this is *the* reason why the pupil is not making the progress for which you had hoped.

4   **Avoid the temptation to label pupils with special needs.** You don't need to label a pupil's difficulties to help them; in fact, using a label can be counterproductive. You may recognize some pupils who seem disadvantaged during all their school career because a label was attached, and both staff and pupils tend to see the pupil through the label.

5   **Don't expect or promise a 'quick fix'.** This can be all the more damaging if you and/or the pupil expect success and progress as a result of 'labelling' the difficulty, but find they are not forthcoming. Labelling does not provide a solution or describe the type of support necessary to meet the pupil's needs. However, it may help you to share a better understanding of the pupil's difficulties.

6   **Stand by for a rush of special needs enquiries after a story in the press or on television.** Popular media coverage of special needs problems to a worried parent or carer can act like a medical dictionary to a hypochondriac! Greater public awareness is a good thing but must be tempered with a rational approach.

7   **Identify what pupils can do well.** Strengths not weaknesses are the key to meeting a pupil's needs. You should look at what you know the pupil needs in order to make progress. You will probably achieve this better if you know what the pupil's strengths are and can use them to meet the needs.

8   **Build up their self-confidence.** Pupils need to have a better opinion of their own personality and ability to improve. You can help to improve that self-image by creating opportunities for success, no matter how small.

9   **Decide whether to proceed further.** How do you know whether the traits you have identified are part of the pattern of one area of difficulty or another? Should you use a particular term to describe areas of difficulty such as Dyslexia or Attention Deficit Disorder? In fact, there are common traits to quite a few named disorders which makes it even more confusing for parent and teacher alike. The Compendium of Special Needs section in this book will give you a number of pointers on identifying special needs to help you to make these difficult decisions.

10   **You don't have to take all the responsibility on your own.** Whether you are a parent, or the SENCO, you cannot be expected to make the assessment alone. You need to know how to find out what to do next, who to contact, where to find advice, and how to go about identifying and providing the right kind of support.

41

Working effectively in the classroom with a peripatetic learning support teacher

If you have pupils in your class who have Statements of Special Educational Needs, it is quite likely that a special support teacher will have been provided to support those pupils in some of your lessons. If this is a new experience for you, the following suggestions may be of use in making the most of this support, both for your pupils and for yourself.

1   **Welcome the support of this teacher in a positive manner.** You may be nervous about having someone in your classroom if you are unused to being observed teaching; it may feel like being a student again! But such a teacher has normally been a classroom teacher, too, and understands what it is like. The role of the support teacher is to help pupils and not to judge your performance. You may learn something, too.

2   **Give some thought as to how you will introduce the support teacher to your class.** Some support teachers prefer to introduce themselves. Be careful to avoid saying something like, 'This is Mrs X and she has come to help James', which may be very embarrassing for the pupil. Instead you can say, 'This is Mrs X who is going to be working with us, so now you have two teachers who can help you with your work'.

3   **Liaise regularly with your support teacher.** It is essential to supply schemes of work for some time ahead to enable the support teacher to devise differentiated material, and also to give some thought to strategies to help needy pupils. Don't just expect them to devise support activities on the hoof.

4   **Use the skills of your support teacher to free you to work on occasions with pupils in need of extra help.** After all, you are often the best person to explain your subject. Organize core work for the class and ask the support teacher to take responsibility for that from time to time, while you work with an individual or small group. Check in advance whether this will be possible.

5   **Use the opportunity to develop partnership teaching.** You could ask the teacher to write key words or draw diagrams on the board while you are speaking. You could also share in the giving of information. A change of voice or style can aid effective teaching. The participation of the support teacher can also be helpful to the supported pupil, and may prevent his or her marginalization. Another advantage of becoming an observer in your own classroom is that you will notice inattention and bad behaviour, which can be overlooked when you are speaking from the front of the classroom.

6   **Give your support to withdrawal of pupils if necessary.** There will be pupils who will need to be withdrawn from your class at certain times. Your permission will be sought as a matter of courtesy, but the decision may have already been taken at a different level. Be gracious in giving consent; your pupil will not benefit if you make your displeasure apparent. This withdrawal may be a crucial or even a statutory feature of support. Perhaps you could arrange for missed work to be photocopied or for your silent reading lesson, or similar activity, to coincide with the withdrawal.

7   **Send positive messages to pupils about support teachers.** Your support teacher may need your help to work effectively in your classroom. Your attitude to this teacher is likely to be crucial, as pupils take their cue from a trusted teacher. Make it clear that you are both professional equals who expect the same standards of behaviour. Show your pupils by words and example that the support teacher is welcome and has authority in the classroom, too.

8   **Give some thought to the practicalities of sharing your classroom.** Is there enough room for the support teacher to circulate comfortably and without disruption? You may need to think about changing seating plans, or moving some pupils from their usual seats without antagonizing them.

9   **Maximize any expertise on offer from your support colleague.** The support teacher is a very expensive resource in your classroom. Are you making the best use of this professional expertise? Remember, this teacher may possess a formidable array of qualifications and experience. If you have, for example, a former head of English in your classroom, make good use of any resources or teaching ideas that are on offer.

10   **Seek outside help if you have problems you cannot solve.** Hopefully you will find that having support with your needy pupils is invaluable. However, if things go wrong and they cannot be resolved amicably between the two of you, it may be necessary to ask the SENCO to mediate or suggest ways in which you could both work in agreement. Be prepared to accept that there is an equal chance that you have some responsibility for any breakdown in working relationships.

42

Identifying special needs: an alphabetical compendium

In the next substantial set of more than a hundred tips, a number of common traits are listed and described in alphabetical order, together with questions and suggestions about how you can begin to meet the pupil's needs. Where it could be helpful, a reference to a broad term into whose category that trait might fit is given, but only because these might help you to identify the people, agencies or kinds of arrangements that could provide the support the pupil needs. This is not meant to act as a system for labelling the pupil, for this could be very dangerous. The pupil's needs are the important thing to remember; distinguishing their strengths from their weaknesses and by so doing, recognizing what specialist help can be sought, is fundamental to meeting the needs of that particular pupil.

Absences

1   **Does the pupil have 'absences'.** Does the pupil appear to simply 'switch off' and go into another world? These can be very short, literally a few seconds, or last longer, perhaps several minutes or so. If they are short, try to ensure, by way of verbal reinforcement for the whole class, that the pupil knows what they missed.

2   **Do you need to do more?** If the absence lasted longer, you will need a more one-to-one situation, where the pupil receives the information missed on an individual verbal basis or with written reinforcement. Try to give this information in diagrammatic or note form for speed.

3   **Help them back gently.** Do not force the pupil back from an absence by shouting at them or confronting them. Avoid any physical contact, even if you are only trying to move the body into an attentive position. Softly spoken, yet firmly repeated words, using the pupil's name may be effective. Possible reasons for absences might include Asperger's

Syndrome, Attention Deficit Disorder, autism (see Chapter 3), or diabetes, epilepsy or other medical conditions, and you will need to seek specialist medical and psychological guidance on whether these are applicable and how you can best support the pupil.

Absenteeism or truancy

4   **Look for patterns.** Does the pupil have long and/or frequent periods of absence from school? Make a note of the times in the term and year when these occur; is there a pattern? Some pupils find it hard to return to a regular pattern of attendance at the beginning of each term, especially if there is no daily pattern at home resulting from parents' hours of work, or whatever.

5   **Probe for the reasons for non-attendance.** Does the pupil seem vague about the reasons for absence? This can often be the case if the parent is supportive of the absences for their own reasons. You will need to work with both parent and pupil on the value of school, so that coming to school is seen to be more positive than being at home or out of school.

6   **Help the pupil get back to regular attendance.** If the pupil is truanting they may be secretive or blatant about it, depending on their personality. Try to establish a set of motivational targets that will encourage the pupil/parent to improve attendance, for example, certificates of achievement at the end of a completed section of work, interesting activities at lunch time or after school, regular verbal and written praise that will increase self-esteem. (See the section in Chapter 1 on school or classroom refusers.)

Antagonism

7   **Is the pupil antagonistic towards all pupils?** If the pupil seems to come into conflict, no matter where and with whom they are, then you know the problem is quite serious. In a secondary school, you can usually tell if it relates to a particular combination of pupils, and that in the company of different pupils this pupil has natural friendships. It is possible that the pupil feels left out, so careful choice of whom to partner them with could change the situation.

8   **Is the pupil antagonistic towards certain pupils?** You will always find that there are instances where pupils become antagonistic towards other particular pupils. It is knowing when and how to distinguish between those instances that are part of the normal ebb and flow of human relationships, and the more deep-seated behavioural attitudes, that is important. As a parent, carer or teacher, you are probably the best judge

of this. Just ask yourself if it has become an expected part of the young person's behaviour? If this is the case, is this more than normal classroom 'ebb and flow'?

9   **Question why the antagonism to certain pupils has arisen.** It can be a form of jealousy, wanting what the other pupil has for example, certain skills, attention from the teacher or kudos with pupils. Perhaps other pupils have made the pupil feel inadequate. Whichever it is, you need to let the pupil know that they have strengths of their own; praise them both openly and quietly to boost their self-esteem.

10 **Is the pupil antagonistic towards those in 'authority'?** Have you noticed that the pupil has a dislike of all teachers and anything which smacks of authority in and around the school? No matter what you say, how reasonable teachers are and how many offers are made for the pupil to discuss their feelings, the pupil remains resentful of anything to do with school. It has become popular to describe this kind of pupil as disaffected. Parents/carers, classroom teachers, special needs teachers and SENCOs will all need to be involved in helping to remediate the problem.

11 **Is the pupil antagonistic towards school as a whole?** In these kinds of cases, no sanction has worked with this pupil, they seem totally turned off. The reason for such behaviour may be too complex for you as an individual to unravel, but if you can find one area of interest that can be developed through one subject area at first and then through others, there may be the chance of change. A whole school approach may be required to establish a timetable that is more appropriate to the pupil's needs; it may be that your school is not the appropriate setting for such a timetable or pupil, in which case, alternatives may need to be explored.

12 **Is the pupil antagonistic towards certain teachers?** Such pupils will often be as disruptive as they can be in lessons, are unconcerned that others cannot learn as a result, and they may well have friends in the lessons who act as an audience. You need to be careful not to play to this audience. It can be best not to respond openly to challenges, to ignore the comments and speak to them quietly, later. (See also the tips contained in Chapter 2, 'Improving unacceptable behaviour'.)

Anti-social behaviour

13   **Does the pupil seem to be a real 'loner' out of choice and actively sits away from other pupils, if space allows, or sits unwillingly with a partner?** All attempts to encourage the pupil to join in with discussion work or activities have met with limited success. It may be that the pupil feels out of place for some reason; this can be very difficult to discuss as it could involve highly personal reasons. If the pupil's progress does not seem affected by this, then it may be best to leave well alone and to talk to specialists who can give appropriate advice.

14   **Accentuate the positive.** If you feel that progress could be considerably improved, tell the pupil what they *are* good at and pinpoint some aspect of work that you think they *will* be good at. Emphasize their strengths, give a feeling of confidence, assure them that you think they can make progress, but that it may come more easily if they could share with other pupils. You may still get nowhere and might need to seek advice. (See also the section in Chapter 1 on 'Strategies to improve low self-esteem in pupils'.)

Attention seeking

15   **Does the pupil try to gain attention from anyone at any time, or can you be more specific about times, places and people?** A general need for attention may be a cry for help, while a specifically related need for attention may be indicative of a skill area with which the pupil has difficulty. If the attention-seeking relates to one particular person, it may be a sign that the pupil would like to be able to talk to that person about other worries.

16   **Be understanding, even with the most 'self-centred' personalities.** You may have no idea until you talk with them how much they have bottled up inside. However, take care, particularly if you are the classroom teacher, not to get too involved; know when to call in professional counselling help.

17   **Encourage the pupil to list the concerns they have.** It helps to put it into perspective. If they can rate the concerns on a scale from 1 to 10, or list areas of their lives which are positive or good, this can also be a step forward. It might be a reassurance to look at the good score ratings and the positive areas as those from which to start building a new approach.

18   **Help them to set individual targets.** Try to ensure you leave the pupil with something they can actively be doing to help themselves. Give them something they are responsible for completing before you next see them.

Attention span

19   **Does the pupil's attention span wander immediately?** Does the pupil seem to have great difficulty focusing on the work in hand? Do they talk about something completely unrelated when asked to get on with the work? You may find they have not understood the instructions or the content of the work so far. Going over the work or instructions with them and simplifying it may help to get them underway.

20   **Does the attention span wander after a while?** Have you noticed that pupils lose interest after ten minutes or so? They probably have a difficulty maintaining concentration and may need to have a change of activity. It can help to set a shorter series of tasks, so that they feel more able to complete them. Keep stretching this list so that they build up a longer span of attention. (See also sections on Attention Deficit Disorder and Attention Deficit Hyperactivity Disorder in Chapter 3.)

Bullying

21   **Is the pupil bullied by others?** You may *not* have noticed that the pupil is bullied; it probably happens outside the classroom, or out of hearing of a teacher. However, it may be that you are aware of comments that are at the expense of a particular pupil. Often other pupils join in the laughter. What may seem just a bit of light hearted fun in isolation, may in fact be part of a wider pattern of picking on that pupil.

22   **Keep an eye on the situation when you suspect bullying.** You may need to ask around. To ask the pupil concerned might make them all the more anxious and embarrassed to talk about it, as if it is their fault. Try to ensure that the pupil is seated where you are able to see and hear. Find out about and follow up the school's policy about bullying. Pupils in these situations need help to build up their own self-esteem. You can help by teaching them strategies that give them confidence to ignore comments or else respond with assurance.

23   **Does the pupil verbally or physically bully other pupils?** Does this continue despite warnings and sanctions? Sometimes this can be the result of having been bullied themselves, but it can be symptomatic of a need the pupil has to feel in control of their life and to feel good about themselves. You can help by talking to them about this and encouraging them to discover the good things about themselves.

24 **Try to distract or deflect bullies.** In the short term you could keep the pupil busy in the lesson, or at breaks, with responsibilities that they feel are special and give them a sense of greater self-esteem. They may become too busy to focus on a weaker pupil.

25 **Work within the school's policy about bullying.** Consistency is all important to building up the pupil's image of themselves. If you can do this, they may no longer feel the need to have control over others. Some schools have a 'no blame' approach, which is designed to prevent repercussions against the bullied pupil and allow the bully a positive starting point.

Calling out

26 **Does the pupil disrupt lessons by calling out questions or comments inappropriately?** This is the pupil who does not mean to be disruptive, but who calls out without waiting turn because they are so eager to please, or who has difficulty storing information and needs to say it while they remember it. The problem is how to respond to this pupil in a way that does not equate them with the pupil who deliberately, defiantly calls out in order to disrupt your lesson. If you are not careful, you will find the disruptive pupil has every right to say that it is unfair when they are treated differently.

27 **Encourage pupils to think before they call out.** It can help if you make it a regular habit that pupils jot down notes as you discuss, or even set time aside and tell them to jot down three or four of their own ideas. Similarly, *before* you ask the question, tell them they must put their hands up if they have an answer. It may help to tell them you know they are waiting to speak so they allow you to listen to another pupil, knowing they are going to be heard.

Cautious pupils

28 **Is the pupil excessively cautious?** Some pupils never like to take any kind of risk and will not venture an answer in case it is wrong, and so never learn to have confidence. They may go away and learn from what others have said, but they could learn more if they were encouraged to try out ideas. You may be able to encourage them by using something that they have written down as an example to the whole class, so that they can see their ideas do have value.

Childishness

29   **Does the pupil behave in a childish manner?** This is not necessarily the same as being immature. Do you recognize the pupil who behaves in a reasonable way most of the time, but on occasions digs their heels in about something quite trivial, in the way that a younger child would? This is not a pupil who is consistently immature. This pupil has what amounts to 'tantrums', and you may be taken by surprise when they happen. You will need to unravel why this happens, and perhaps address it directly with the pupil on a one-to-one basis.

30   **Childish behaviour requires sympathetic adult handling.** The pupil's response is often irrational and they get all the more worked up because of that. It may be best if you avoid trying to rationalize with them in that state of mind, but try diverting the attention to another task and follow up afterwards.

Clumsiness

31   **Is your pupil excessively clumsy?** You probably recognize the pupil who manages to drop books, knock pens and equipment off a desk, bumps into furniture and pupils as they are working, breaks things accidentally and has great difficulty with skills requiring coordination, such as ruling a straight line, underlining words and drawing a graph. This may or may not be an indicator of a special need, so monitor the situation and if concerned, discuss it with others.

32   **Try not to be overtly critical of clumsiness.** This pupil needs a lot of patience and understanding, and will probably be deeply aware (and often ashamed) of the problem. Repeatedly telling them to look at what they are doing will only cause more frustration at their own lack of skill.

33   **Try minimizing the 'clutter' around them, including their own, so that they can have space in which to move about successfully.** Let them focus on one task at a time, allow time for underlining work, drawing columns, and so on. Don't move on until they are ready; if you do, the problems are likely to begin to pile up and overlap each other.

Copying problems

34 **Think about why some pupils copy work down more slowly than others.** There are some who have great difficulty copying work correctly, and who are so much slower than other pupils completing this exercise. The temptation is to move on before they have finished the work because others are sitting waiting. If you do this, the pupil will always be behind and cannot value your subject.

35 **Try to organize your activities so that there is an extension piece of work to keep the quicker ones focused on the topic.** It can help the pupil if they are trained to read a short phrase from the text and keep repeating it in their head as they copy it, then move to the next phrase. This way they get away from the tendency to look at each word separately and copy down one word at a time. It also helps to add meaning to what they write.

36 **Reduce the text to a minimum for those pupils with severe short-term visual memory.** They probably do need to look at each letter in a word, but again if they can be encouraged to sound the word out in their head, letter by letter until the word becomes familiar, they have more chance of overcoming this eventually. (See also the section on 'Multi-sensory teaching strategies' in Chapter 1.)

Defensiveness

37 **Be aware that excessive defensiveness may be an indicator of another underlying problem.** You will know of some pupils who always assume that they are being criticized and quickly defend whatever it is they think they are being criticized for. It may be that they expect to be criticized, because they have real feelings of inadequacy and need to have their self-esteem boosted.

38 **Try to make a point of getting them to *recognize* the positive things you say about them.** When you praise them, make sure they understand that it is praise. If necessary, reinforce this with a tangible recognition of their good points, for example, a sticker or merit mark. Praise them in front of other pupils and staff. (See also sections in Chapter 2, 'Improving unacceptable behaviour'.)

Defiance

39 **Discriminate between defiance and aggression.** A defiant pupil is not exactly the same as the aggressive pupil, but may have many behavioural similarities. The difference may be in the degree to which they seek out attention. The defiant pupil may have been subdued until requested to do something, then they refuse. The aggressive pupil has probably already been disruptive. Aggression is more proactive, defiance is more reactive.

40 **Take a proactive stance.** You are more likely to have success if you have pre-empted their reaction, maybe even made a start on the activity jointly as a class, so that they are already underway. Sometimes, it is because they feel insecure about how to proceed, they kick up a fuss rather than lose face.

Examination phobia

41 **Look out for pupils with extreme reactions to exams.** Some pupils suffer from extreme stress when facing examinations, far stronger than the normal anxiety we all feel at times. These may leave the pupil unable to write coherently (or even at all), and may result in the pupil failing to turn up for important public exams. Very often the pupil will be extremely able and will have prepared conscientiously for the exam.

42 **Take the issue seriously.** In the best cases, the problem will have surfaced soon enough for the pupil to have received some exam anxiety counselling and strategic advice to help overcome the problem. It is important to act when this rather uncommon syndrome occurs, since the consequences of ignoring it can be serious.

Excessively critical pupils

43 The pupil who is critical of others, of what is being taught or of themselves, has often grown used to critical comments as a way of life, either at home or in relation to their work in school. Remember, everyone needs to hear good things. Try to turn their critical comments around, so that they have a positive meaning and build from there.

Handwriting problems

44 **Recognize that poor handwriting is a widespread problem.** There are very few pupils who don't have handwriting problems at some stage, and even teachers are not exempt! How many pupils have you heard say they can't read what the teacher has written? The crucial issue with poor handwriting is how early it is identified. It could be a mistake to try to change a pupil's handwriting once they are into external examination situations, for example, Year 9 and SATs, Year 10 and 11 and GCSEs.

45 **Look for ways to remediate problems.** If caught early enough, you can attempt to reintroduce style to the writing, for example, cursive, joined writing. You may be able to alter the pen grip (special pens can be bought which are shaped to improve grip). If this is too late, try identifying the individual problems, for example, keeping on the line, spacing between words, clarity of letter shapes. A motto, such as, 'Line, Space, Shape' repeated in the head or on a card, can help to focus on improvement.

Hyperactivity

46 **Hyperactive pupils cannot stay still or quiet, no matter what anyone does.** Often you will find they stand at their desk or workspace or, at the very least, kneel on their chair. You may find that changing activity for this pupil more frequently than for others helps them to stay still. If you give them a responsibility between activities, which allows them to move about, they may satisfy their need for movement.

47 **Set short term targets of keeping on task for five minutes or so and then increasing them can also prove successful.** You could try to make the breaks between tasks a further way of motivating them. This could be when they earn praise, some reward for completing the tasks. (See also the section on 'Attention Hyperactivity Deficit Disorder' in Chapter 3.)

Hypochondria

48 **Take pupils seriously when they tell you about medical concerns.** When a pupil spends a lot of time worrying about illnesses, or confides in you about symptoms they think they have, this is a cause for concern. It may be that they have genuine problems, or they may be excessively anxious or stressed about other things that they are trying to bring to your attention in this way.

49   **Try to find some way of reassuring them.** Don't dismiss their worries without really listening, or ignore what they have said, they may end up worrying more. Try to reassure them with a reasoned answer they can understand.

50   **Follow this by diverting their attention to some activity they will enjoy.** Their worries may stem from problems elsewhere, from news about relatives or friends that they find hard to understand. It may even be that they want the attention someone else they know is getting because they are ill.

51   **Know when to refer the matter on.** If the complaints and anxieties continue for several weeks, it might be advisable to discuss it with the school counsellor or school nurse (if you have one), the family and other specialists, who may ask the advice of the pupil's doctor.

Immaturity

52   **Watch out for pupils who are 'out of synch' with their peers.** Every so often you do come across a pupil who does not cope with friendships in their own year group, and who becomes isolated because of their immature behaviour. They may be prone to tantrums, make silly, irrelevant comments in class, seek you out to talk to at break times because they can't socialize with their peers. You will need to be firm but understanding.

53   **Help them to avoid being marked out by peers as a 'baby'.** They may still have obvious habits from childhood, such as sucking their thumb, keeping a 'comforter' in their bag, always bringing things to show you, or telling tales about others in the class. One way forward might be to isolate one of these features of behaviour which irritates their peers, and concentrate on encouraging them to grow out of it. This could be helped by diverting their attention to other interests. Try to find one interest they have which is shared by a more mature pupil.

54   **Involve parents and carers.** It may be that the family needs support dealing with this area of difficulty, although it may not have been noticed at home if there are no older children or if other siblings are equally immature. You may discover the pupil has continued to have their own way by throwing tantrums. You may need to offer this pupil the motivation to grow up by rewarding progress, not tantrums. The best reward should be acceptance by peers and involvement in peer activities.

Insecurity

55 **Help pupils to recognize that insecurity is not uncommon.** Most of us have experienced this at some time, particularly when we move school or job. For insecure pupils though, the slightest change to a routine can leave them worried. They may linger at the end of a lesson if they are anxious about something, perhaps the next lesson, and yet wait for you to say something. Reassure them that nothing awful will happen, but try to make a point of seeing them later to reinforce the fact that nothing went wrong.

56 **Help them find paths to security.** They may hide in the safety of a larger group, and if told to do something on their own, ask if their friend can help them. You could give them some responsibility, which will give them confidence, particularly one which means that others will look to them for a sense of security, perhaps fixing the time and date for a class activity. It will be important that they gain success here, but equally important that they should realize that even if something goes wrong, it is not the end of the world.

57 **Reassure, but don't treat them as infantile.** They will often double check with you the detail of some task they have been asked to do, or repeatedly check details of dates, times and places. You can help them acquire a greater sense of security by writing things down, so that they can definitely check details and not rely on their memory. It may be therapeutic for them to realize that it is better to try something, even risk something, than never to have attempted it in the first place.

Jokers

58 **Look for the reasons why the joker has to make everything into a cause of laughter.** Sometimes you come across the pupil who cannot take anything seriously and jokes about everything. They have often become the class clown and others expect them to entertain. The reasons behind this behaviour can be various; the able pupil who is bored and, rather than be seen as over studious, prefers to make light of their ability; the pupil who feels out of their depth and covers this up by joking about it.

59 **Find out what you can about what is going on.** You do need to have some knowledge of the reason for the behaviour before you can persuade the pupil that there is a time and place for everything. If it is part of a wider problem to do with self-esteem, then try to talk to other staff; you may be able to find ways in which the pupil may be more stretched or not so out of their depth in their lessons.

60   **Be careful about changing the butt of the joke.** A pupil who jokes, generally likes others laughing *with* them. Try to avoid putting an end to it by making other pupils laugh *at* them. If you can put an end to the joking in a light-hearted way yourself, then you are more likely to be successful in diverting the pupil's attention back to work.

Left-handedness

61   **Consider the needs of left-handed pupils.** Of course, being left-handed is not a learning difficulty in itself and should not be treated as a problem. However, as one in seven pupils is left-handed, we need to take account of their needs by, for example, providing left-handed scissors where these are needed for class work. It can help also to ensure that left-handed pupils are seated on the left of right-handed pupils when written work is taking place to avoid crowding. Specialist shops exist to supply left-handed equipment, and these could be worth investigating for practical subjects.

ME (Myalgic Encephalomyelitis)

62   **Offer academic and physical support to pupils with ME.** This is more commonly known as chronic fatigue syndrome, or post-viral syndrome, and the medical profession is still divided about the causes and nature of this condition. Pupils with ME present can have debilitating symptoms; they may need a wheelchair for some periods of time; they may suffer from sustained absences from school, or the ability to cope only with part-time schooling. They need support in several dimensions.

Memory problems

63   **Distinguish between absentmindedness and genuine memory problems.** We all suffer from memory problems at times, which can become more pronounced under stress. Some pupils are so disorganized, they find it even harder to remember basic information. Pupils like this often have a general difficulty remembering to bring equipment to a lesson. Others may have more specific difficulty remembering things they have seen or heard, in which case they probably have visual or auditory short-term memory difficulties.

64   **Determine in which area the pupil has the memory problem.** You will be able to help the pupil more effectively if you do so. If they are disorganized, try to set up a system for them of reminder notes and notices, both at home and in school. If they find it hard remembering what has been said, then use visual cues to reinforce the information. If they find it hard to recall something visual, then explain it in words as well. (See also sections on 'Dyslexia' and 'Dyspraxia' in Chapter 3.)

Moodiness

65 **Watch out for pupils who have mood swings.** This is often a sign of something troubling the pupil, which in turn may have led to sleepless nights and irritability. There may be particular occasions, or references to topics in school, that set off the mood. Try to make a note of these, and be particularly supportive towards the pupil.

66 **If you perceive any patterns, consider talking about it to the pupil.** You might be able to help them talk about the reason behind the moods if you approach it sensitively, saying that you have noticed times when they seem unhappy. If the moodiness is actually preventing the pupil from making progress, then you might need to speak to the parents or discuss this with the school's Educational Welfare Officer.

Muscular dystrophy

67 **Be aware of the varying needs of pupils with muscular dystrophy.** This is a genetically inherited, degenerative, muscle-wasting disease for which the long term prognosis is very poor. Many children with this condition opt to pursue their education in a special school, but others may wish to stay as long as possible in a mainstream school. Their needs will vary according to the stage of progress of the condition.

68 **Consider mobility issues.** Some pupils may still be able to walk, but may need help climbing stairs, negotiating busy parts of the school, or getting up out of chairs. Others may be wheelchair users and will need help with lifts. There are also special typewriters available for use when hands are not functioning very effectively, and as these pupils will have Statements of Special Educational Needs, there is also likely to be academic and auxiliary support available.

Nervousness

69 **Be really sensitive about making nervous pupils feel exposed.** They may find it very difficult to perform in front of others, whether it involves reading aloud, answering a question, or demonstrating something. If you force this pupil ,you may make things worse, particularly if they lose face during the performance. It might be better to ask for volunteers, and 'engineer' with a friend of the pupil that they volunteer to try something together. If this works, gradually wean the pupil away from needing the 'supporting act'.

Obsessive behaviour

70 **Be aware of signs of obsessive behaviour.** There are some pupils who, for a number of different reasons, may display obsessive behaviours. You may recognize that these range from rocking to and fro in their chair, to repeatedly dismantling pieces of equipment, or chewing at their cuffs. Sometimes these are ways of comforting themselves with a familiar routine, but for those who are absorbed by the activity and who become agitated if they are prevented from continuing, these can be signs of other problems. Remember, however, that irritating habits do not always constitute obsessive behaviour!

71 **Use a light touch.** The pupil may be trying to blot out what they cannot cope with by becoming completely occupied with something else. If you remove the 'obsession' you may create extreme anxieties. Try not to take away the 'obsession' completely, show an interest and try to arrange a time when they can legitimately return to the activity. In the meantime, without their 'prop,' they may need your support all the more. (See sections on 'Autism' and 'Asperger's Syndrome' in Chapter 3.)

Outbursts

72 **Recognize the difference between over-enthusiastic participation and an outburst.** This is different from the pupil who calls out, who may be trying to answer a question. This pupil wants to draw attention to themselves, and not just from you. They can be looking for any excuse to achieve this. These occasions have a volatile nature, and responding to this with raised voice or sharp words may simply fuel their outburst to even greater heights.

73 **Try to diffuse the situation by assuring the pupil that you know there must have been a problem for them to have reacted as they did.** Talk quietly and calmly to avoid the rash response; you will be surprised how often this can settle a 'hot-head' down and they lower their voice and slow the pace down. (See Chapter 2 on 'Improving unacceptable behaviour'.)

Post-traumatic shock disorder

74 **Seek out ways to support pupils who have experienced serious trauma.** This is most likely in schools which shelter large numbers of refugee children. In extreme cases, some children will actually have arrived in this country alone and without adult support. They may have seen their parents killed in extremely brutal ways. They may have lived in constant fear of attack and death, and may have experienced great personal physical and emotional trauma. In the past, we might have described these children as 'shell-shocked'. They will need all the support you can give them in the classroom, as well as long-term professional support.

Questioning everything

75 **Try to work out why the pupil is doing it.** The pupil who always asks questions can be a frustrated able pupil, who needs to know more than you or a teacher has told them. On the other hand, this could be a pupil who thinks they are always right and likes to argue and win. There is also the pupil who argues for the sake of it, so that it disrupts the lesson. You will probably know which of these three your pupil is.

76 **Avoid rising to the bait or losing your temper.** Try to answer the question reasonably, no matter what you think is the motive; that way you can't be accused by the pupil of not treating them fairly. If the pupil is gifted, then offer some extension work that satisfies the enquiring mind. If it is the argument the pupil enjoys, then engage in a short discussion before suggesting they write down their argument. In itself, the need to question or argue is not significant, but it may be part of a wider pattern.

Quiet pupils

77 **Try to draw out quiet pupils in lessons, particularly by pairing them with a partner.** These young people can often go unnoticed in class because they never ask questions, never volunteer answers, don't talk to a neighbour and don't cause any problems. They usually don't want to be noticed, and the worry about this is that you may not be aware when they have a difficulty. If you discover that they are not this quiet at home, then it might be an idea to talk to them about any worries they have in school.

Rudeness

78 **Set ground rules with rude pupils.** You may feel that you come across more pupils who are simply rude and have no manners. However, this kind of pupil does not seem to have respect for others, and yet if someone is rude to them they are quick to complain. It may be that they simply do not know what is expected of them, and that they talk in the way they have been allowed to. It may be that they do know how to behave respectfully, but deliberately want to defy this.

79 **Don't give rude pupils the satisfaction of you rising to the bait and responding in kind.** Raising your voice to this pupil may only serve to fuel them into saying more, or using swear words more freely.

80 **Try to ensure that however you react, you do it within the school's policy for behaviour.** Try to be calm, no matter what the pupil has called you or said to you, but tell them they need to think and be careful about what they say. Be firm, let them know you have a clear standard of behaviour and that you will not accept certain kinds of behaviour, no matter what.

81 **Investigate possible reasons for rudeness.** Try to find out from others if something else has just happened, perhaps in the previous lesson which has contributed to the ill-mannered behaviour.

Reading difficulties

82 **Keep a watching brief for pupils who don't read well.** This is probably the most common of the difficulties you might notice in a pupil. It should be possible to tell this pupil apart from the one who is nervous when reading aloud. This pupil will have great difficulty building up word sounds, and may make wild guesses at words based on the first letter only.

83 **Try to provide reading materials at an appropriate level.** You need to know what reading age this pupil operates at, and check the readability levels of the texts this pupil is expected to read. You can help most by ensuring the pupil has texts that they can read; they will not progress if faced with failure and they need to know they can gain success.

84 **Find out if it is possible to provide structured support.** If the pupil's reading age is behind the chronological age by two years or more, then it seems likely that such a pupil would benefit from some programme of reading support. You should consider seeking or providing this on a daily basis. Such regular reinforcement will help them to recall patterns and improve fluency.

Self-mutilation and self-harm

85 **Be aware of the potential for pupils to hurt themselves.** These tendencies are clearly a sign of deep distress and confusion. The sufferers are mainly (although not exclusively) girls. They may cut or damage themselves, persistently pull out their hair or seek ways to make themselves as unattractive as possible. In extreme cases, some pupils may make clumsy suicide attempts in an attempt to draw attention to their distress. Such pupils are also likely to suffer from low self-esteem. Their safety and security must be a priority, but long-term solutions will be needed to help them feel better about themselves.

Sensory impairment

86 **Be sensitive to the needs of pupils with sensory impairments.** These may include impairment of sight, hearing and speech. Teachers may be involved in using equipment, such as two-way hearing aids or magnifying equipment, to make text more accessible. Pupils may need extra support, both from staff who are experts in this field and from mainstream teachers, in order to get full access to the curriculum.

Sequencing difficulties

87 **Give help to those who find it hard to get things in the right order.** Some pupils have enormous difficulties getting things in the right order, whether it is a series of instructions you have given them or the order of letters in a word. You may be able to help them if you can train them to repeat instructions in their head, so that the order is filed away more effectively in the memory. Similarly, you could give them a series of prompt cards that help them to recall the correct sequence for something.

88 **Work out how best to help sequencing.** They may have this difficulty only when working orally or it may occur with written/visual ideas. You can help them if you give things in their correct order, rather than adding on afterthoughts which confuse. Avoid saying, 'But before you do this…' as this means you have given out the information in the wrong order. Use their areas of strength, for example, visual or auditory. (See sections on 'Dyslexia' in Chapter 3 and 'Multi-sensory teaching' in Chapter 1.)

Sexually inappropriate behaviour

89   **Watch out for the signs of sexually inappropriate behaviour.** This may embrace a range of behaviour, which includes exposure of genitalia to other cases, or even in extreme cases, masturbation. Obviously, this is a pretty strong indicator of a troubled and confused child in need of help and counselling. Another manifestation of sexually inappropriate behaviour is the use of sexually explicit language, or even sexually explicit role play involving other pupils. The pupil may write or draw in an inappropriate manner in the course of school work. This kind of behaviour may also be a possible indication of sexual abuse. Whatever the cause, the child is in need of help and referral to professional expertise.

90   **Be supportive to all concerned.** Classroom teachers will need to be supportive, both to the acting-out child and those affected by this behaviour. (See also the section on 'Physical, emotional or sexual abuse' in Chapter 3.)

Short concentration span

91   **Differentiate between short concentration and short attention span.** There is a fine difference between the two. The concentration span is the length of time that the pupil works most effectively at the topic, before they lose enthusiasm or commitment and the work drops in quality. When the attention also deteriorates, the pupil is no longer on task at all. You could help by ensuring that a task can be completed in blocks of time that are within the pupil's concentration span.

92   **Ensure that the really vital areas of the work are conveyed in a direct, immediately accessible way.** If the task can be broken down into discrete areas, try to encourage a fresh start or approach for each area. You may motivate this pupil more by presenting this change of approach, rather than giving more of the same.

Slow responses

93   **Be aware that some students work much more slowly than others.** Some pupils have difficulties processing information quickly and respond later than other pupils; you may notice they can become the butt of jokes as a result. This can be particularly painful for them in oral work. These pupils may find it easier to write down ideas, rather than formulate and hold information in their heads.

Speech difficulties

94 **Identify those pupils who don't find it easy to speak.** Pupils with speech difficulties often have great difficulty communicating effectively with others. You probably recognize the pupil who has difficulty chatting easily, or whose speech is difficult to understand, who uses immature sentences, 'switches off' frequently or says little to anyone. If the pupil has this level of difficulty communicating to others, then it is possible they may have an equal difficulty understanding what is said to them.

95 **Build in successes along the way for pupils who find it hard to talk, so that they know they are making progress.** You need to be very supportive of this pupil and work with them on a one-to-one basis. Let them know that you are there to help them bridge the gap between what they understand and what they have to communicate.

Spelling difficulties

96 **Try to identify why pupils have difficulties with spelling.** Many people have spelling difficulties and sometimes it is just carelessness, the result of trying to write too fast. For some pupils though, it is a real problem and they really have no method or strategies for improving their spelling. These pupils do not have an in-built sense of what looks or feels right as they write a word. You can help them most by creating a system that will help them.

97 **Give pupils guidelines and support so they can improve their spelling.** You can help them by suggesting a series of subject-specific words on handy cards for reference, or a series of cards with most commonly used or misspelt words, cards with word families that are tricky, and so on. However, they may benefit most from a structured programme of spelling patterns that will familiarize them with certain rules and tips for remembering spellings, such as mnemonics. (See also section 35.)

Stutters

98 **Find out the extent of the problem.** Parents can be more concerned about the pupil who stutters than the pupil is, so as parents/carers and teachers you need to monitor the problem and judge how severe it is. The pupil may only stutter occasionally, or it may be combined with other speech difficulties. The pupil may get irritated by their impediment, or become self-conscious if taunted by other pupils. You need to know how the pupil responds and be aware of other pressures that may relate to the problem.

99   **Help the stutterer to cope with the problem.** It can help the pupil more if you don't finish what they are saying when they get stuck on one word or sound; let them decide for themselves when they need the help. Try to avoid asking the pupil to repeat too much of what they have said. If they volunteer to speak aloud, encourage them and return to them later as a sign of approval that they have done well.

Telling lies repeatedly

100   **Work out whether lying is an indication of a special need.** Pupils and adults tell lies for many different reasons, but it does not mean they have a special needs problem. However, if you know a pupil perpetually tells lies, it may be a form of attention seeking. If you never know when they are lying, but know that they use lies to cover up something, then it could be related to behavioural difficulties to which they refuse to admit.

Tired pupils

101   **Find out why they are tired.** A pupil who seems to be tired on a regular basis may have difficulties outside school that you should try to find out about, particularly if they seem to be finding their schoolwork more difficult to handle as a result. It could just be a growing phase they are going through, but it could also be that they need help.

102   **Seek out specific reasons.** Maybe they have an after or before school job that is just too much for them, perhaps they are going to bed very late. Some children are too scared to go to sleep for fear of something unpleasant happening, or because they have watched something unsuitable on television or video. You need to find out the reason, especially if they are actually falling asleep in school. The tiredness could also be linked to some medication or substance they are taking. You should speak to their Head of Year or form tutor before seeking advice on what to do next.

Withdrawn pupils

103   **Seek out the reasons for withdrawal.** Some pupils are very withdrawn, even to the extent that they may have become school refusers. If you are the teacher, you cannot help them if they are not present in school, so you do need to work with the family and the School's Educational Welfare Officer to manage a return to school. Try to find out if there are particular lessons, pupils or points in the day that the pupil cannot face.

104 **Plan with them how they can cope with the situation.** If necessary, be there to support them. You may find that the pupil can tell you what they would like to change, if they could. Try to follow up on this, and show them that you have listened and have made alternative arrangements where appropriate.

105 **Encourage withdrawn pupils to become more resilient.** Through your help, they can eventually come to school without relying on the support to get them through the day. Discuss this with them, but assure them you will help to ensure that all teachers work at their pace. It may help if you give them the responsibility of telling you when they are ready to change the situation.

Information Section

UK

Kidscape is a registered charity (Charity No. 326864) in the UK
Address: KIDSCAPE
152 Buckingham Palace Road, London SWIW 9TR.
Tel 0171 730 3300; Fax 0171 730 7081
Services provided:
Kidscape Helpline for Parents of Bullied Pupils
Mon–Fri, 10am–4pm 0171 730 3300
Pupil's Legal Centre Helpline
Mon–Fri 2–5 pm 01206 873820

Counselling:
PupilLine for pupils only 0800 1111
ParentLine local contact numbers on 01702 559900
Youth Access: details of young people's counsellors
throughout the country 0181 772 9900

EXEL (Producers of writing frames)
EXEL Project, EXEL Office, Exeter University School of Education,
Heavitree Road, Exeter EX1 2LU

Refugee Council
3 Bondway, London SW8 1SJ
Tel 0171 582 6922
Services and publications: list of regional refugee groups and community
organizations

SMILE: the Secondary Maths Individualized Learning Experience
The SMILE Centre, Isaac Newton Centre, 108a, Lancaster Road, London W11
1QS

Canada

Canadian Child Care Federation
120 Holland Avenue, #306, Ottawa, Ontario, K1Y 0X6
Tel: (613) 729 5269; Fax (613) 729 3158

Child Find Canada
710 Dorval Drive, #508 Oakville, Ontario, L6K 3V7
Tel (905) 845 3463; Fax (905) 845 9621

Canadian Institute of Child Health
855 Meadowlands Drive East, #512, Ottawa, Ontario, K2C 3N2
Tel (613) 224 4144; Fax (613) 224 4152

At this same address are some affiliates, such as
Canadian Coaltion for the Prevention of Developmental Disabilities
Early Childhood Educators of BC

Kids Help Foundation
439 University Avenue, #300, Toronto, Ontario, M5G 1Y8
Tel (416) 586 0100 ext 249; Fax (416) 586 1880
(this organization runs a national phone-in line for kids in need)

Association Canadienne de la Dyslexia
1774 Kerry Avenue, Ottawa, Ontario
Tel (613) 729 3844; Fax (613) 729 4969

Learning Disabilities Association of Canada
Troubles d'Apprentissage – Association Canadienne
323 Chapel Street, Suite 200, Ottawa, Ontario, K1N 7Z2
Tel (613) 238 5721; Fax (613) 235 5391

New Zealand

Commissioner for Children
PO Box 12–537, Wellington

Health and Disability Commissioner
PO Box 1791, Auckland

Early Childhood Development Unit
PO Box 5290, Dunedin

Special Education Services
Public Trust Building, 442 Moray Place, PO Box 5147, Dunedin

References

The following books are ones we have found useful.

Adams, F J (1990) *Special Education in the 1990s*, Longman Industry and Public Service Management, Longman, Harlow.

Allen, B (1993) *Children in Control*, Lucky Duck Publishing ISBN 1 873942 65 6.

Besag, V (1989) *Bullies and Victims in Schools*, OU Press, Buckingham.

Caswell, J and Pinner S (eds) *SENA+T, Special Educational Needs Assistants and Teachers*, Northumberland County Council Education Department.

Curle, J (1995) *Basic Skills Support in School: a guide for every teacher*, Basic Skills Agency.

DfEE (1994) *The Code of Practice; on Identification and Assessment of Special Educational Needs*.

DfEE (1997) *Excellence for All Children*; Green Paper.

Freeman, A and Gray, H (1989) *Organising Special Educational Needs: a critical approach*, Paul Chapman Publishing, London.

Hartley, R L (1986) 'Imagine you're clever', *Journal of Child Psychology and Psychiatry*.

Lawrence, D (1973) *Improved Reading through Counselling*, Ward Lock, London.

Lawrence, D (1988) *Enhancing Self-Esteem in the Classroom*, Paul Chapman Publishing Ltd, London.

Lawrence, D (1996) 2nd edition *Enhancing Self-Esteem in the Classroom*, Paul Chapman Publishing Ltd, London.

Lewis, M and Wray D (1995) *Children Writing Non-fiction*, Scholastic Publications, Leamington Spa.

McCarthy, D and Davies J (1995), *The Practical SEN Resource Manual for Teachers implementing The Code of Practice*, Specialist Matters.

McNamara, S and Morton, G (1995) *Changing Behaviour*, David Fulham Publishers, London.

Patteson, K, Coltheart, M and Marshall, J (eds) (1985) *Surface Dyslexia*, Lawrence Erlbaum Associates, London.

Tatton, D and Lane, D (1989) *Bullying in Schools*, Tentham Books, London.

Webster, A, Beveridge, M C and Reed, M (1996) *Managing the Literacy Curriculum: how schools can become communities of readers and writers*, Routledge, London.

Wray, D and Lewis, M (1997) *Extending Literacy*, Routledge, London.

Glossary

Asperger's Syndrome. This is regarded as part of the autism continuum; it is a speech and language disorder in which the child has autistic tendencies, but appears to have more normal intelligence and communication skills.

Attention Deficit Disorder (ADD). This is a term applied to children who have severe difficulties with attention span and impulse control, and is regarded as a behavioural problem which may stem from a medical condition.

Attention Deficit Hyperactivity Disorder (ADHD) is a further category of ADD in which the child also displays hyperactivity. Together they form a continuum, and assessment needs to include the views of doctors, psychologists and teachers.

Autism is a speech and language communication disorder in which the child has difficulties relating to people, speech and responding to their environment.

Cloze work is a procedure to enable pupils to write sentences by means of providing blank spaces in the text to be filled in from a word bank on the same page.

Code of Practice. The Code of Practice in the UK is a government document published in 1995, which gives advice to LEAs and schools about their respective responsibilities for pupils with special educational needs. There are five stages in the Code of Practice; the first three stages are in-school responsibility for provision. Stage 4 is where the LEA take responsibility for a Formal Statutory Assessment of the needs (FSA), and at Stage 5 the LEA issue a Statement of Special Educational Needs for the pupil. Support for the pupil may now be sought from the Authority.

Differentiation is the term applied to the process of making every aspect of work, from reading texts and worksheets to activities, suitable for the needs of individual pupils.

Disapplied status. Some pupils, with particularly severe learning difficulties, may be disapplied from the UK National Curriculum or parts of it, including the Key Stage Tests. This means they do not need to follow the same courses and subjects taught to those who take the full National Curriculum, including the Key Stage tests.

Dyslexia. The Code of Practice describes pupils who are dyslexic as, 'having significant difficulties in reading, writing, spelling or manipulating numbers, which are not typical of their general level of performance'.

Dyspraxia. This may be described as an impairment of the organization of movement and coordination, which can also affect language perception and thought.

Emotional and Behavioural Difficulties (EBD). This term covers a wide range of difficulties. These may be displayed in various forms: being withdrawn, depressive or obsessional, having phobias, misusing substances, demonstrating disruptive behaviour, anger and violence. These might result from sensory or physical impairment, psychological problems, or physical or mental illness.

General Certificate in Secondary Education (GCSE). At present in England pupils take examinations in Core Subjects (English, Maths, Science, Modern Foreign Language, Technology). They are allowed to take further Option Subjects (History, Geography, Music, Drama PE, RE, etc).

Global Learning Difficulties. This is a term used to describe pupils who might have difficulties in most of the following areas of their development: communication skills, self-help skills, social development skills, emotional and behavioural skills, concept development, the acquisition of basic literacy and numeracy skills, mobility skills. This term is used to describe children who have a general level of attainment that is significantly below that of their peers.

Hearing Impairment (HI). Hearing Impairment affects a significant proportion of children and may be temporary or permanent. Temporary hearing losses are usually caused by 'glue ear' and can be mild or moderate. They can compound other learning difficulties. Permanent hearing losses are usually sensory-neural, and vary from mild, through moderate to severe or profound. A formal statutory assessment leading to a Statement of Special Needs is likely to be required for profound and severe losses and may be required for moderate losses.

IEPs. Individual Educational Plans are taken from Statements of Special Needs where the pupil concerned has been Statemented, and normally including targets, measurable outcomes and causes for concern.

Key Stage Tests. There are four Key Stages in the UK at which pupils following the National Curriculum are tested on their understanding of its content. Key Stage 1 tests pupils in Primary school in Year 2; Key Stage 2 tests pupils in Primary school in Year 6; Key Stage 3 tests pupils in Secondary School in Year 9; Key Stage 4 test pupils in Secondary School in Year 11. The tests at Key Stage 4 are better known as GCSEs.

Learning Difficulty. Pupils are deemed to have a learning difficulty if they have significantly greater difficulty in learning than the majority of children of the same age, or if a disability prevents or hinders them from making use of educational facilities of the kind provided for other children of the same age.

Learning Support Assistants (LSAs). In the UK, learning support assistants are employed by the Local Authority or by the school in areas where this responsibility has been devolved to the schools. The support assistants support pupils with Statements of Special Educational Needs, but they may also be in support for pupils at lower stages of the Code of Practice. Their role is as a non-teaching assistant, but the Government Green Paper (1997) points the way to opening more opportunities for training for support assistants.

Learning Support Teacher. A peripatetic teacher, employed by the Local Authority Learning Support Service, to provide specialized support in mainstream schools for pupils with Statements of Special Educational Needs. These teachers are experienced mainstream teachers who have additional qualifications and experience in a wide range of specific learning difficulties. Their services were formerly funded by the Local Authority in the UK and allocated to schools on the basis of need, but are now generally purchased by schools from their own budgets with the Learning Support Service acting as both employer and agency.

Office for Standards in Education (Ofsted). In the UK, this is the body charged with the responsibility for assuring quality and standards in schools.

Physical Disabilities. These can be the result of illness, injury or a congenital condition. Short and long-term consequences can result. Pupils may also have sensory impairments, neurological conditions and learning difficulties. Appropriate provision will depend on many factors; medical involvement, access to the curriculum, growing discrepancy between the child's ability and their attainment, level of supervision required and emotional factors. Where the physical disability arises suddenly, resulting from an accident, operation or illness, contingency provision may be made available.

SATs: Standard Assessment Tests are the tests used in the UK at the end of each Key Stage in a pupil's career to test understanding of the National Curriculum.

Special Educational Needs (SEN). A pupil who has Special Educational Needs is recognized as having a learning difficulty.

Special Educational Needs Co-ordinator (SENCO). Under the UK Code of Practice, every school should have a SENCO. This named person is often the Head of Special Educational Needs Department or Head of the Learning Support Department, but this does not have to be the case. The SENCO is responsible for identifying pupils with SEN and managing the provision of support for them.

Specific Learning Difficulties (SpLD). Pupils with Specific Learning Difficulties have difficulties in reading, writing, spelling or number work, which is not typical of their general level of performance. They may gain competence in some subject area skills quickly and with a high level of oral ability, but they may have continued difficulty in gaining literacy and numeracy skills.

SMILE : Secondary Maths Individualized Learning Experience (see Information Section).

Statement of Special Educational Needs. This is drawn up by the Local Education Authority following advice given by all interested parties. The Statement sets out the pupil's needs and objectives for education. It also indicates the provision required to meet these objectives. This constitutes Stage Five of the Code of Practice in the UK.

Visual Impairment (VI). Visual difficulties cover a range of minor and remedial conditions to complete blindness. Pupils can be born blind, lose their sight resulting from injury or progressive illness. The degree and nature of vision the child has is crucial to the provision required. Formal statutory assessment may be required for pupils who have some levels of functional vision, and are likely to be required for a pupil who is registered blind or who is expected to go blind.

Writing Frames. Skeleton outlines on which to scaffold children's non-fiction writing using key words and phrases.

Index

DATE DUE

362.1 Fiv
500 Tips for working with
children with special needs
$15.00 13/30/2010 885938

Breinigsville, PA USA
21 September 2010
245795BV00004B/42/A

9 780749 427894